THERE

×

"Elsewhere: There"
Various
First Published 2012

Published by Cargo Publishing & McSweeney's
978-1-908885-06-7

Bic Code-FA Modern & Contemporary Fiction
FYB Short Stories

Published in association with the Edinburgh International Book Festival,
with the support of Creative Scotland and the Scottish Government's
Edinburgh Festivals Expo Fund.

Also available as:
Ebook
Kindle ebook

Printed & bound in China by Shanghai Offset Printing Products Ltd.
Cover illustrations by Jack Teagle
Designed by McSweeney's

www.cargopublishing.com
www.mcsweeneys.net
www.edbookfest.co.uk
www.jackteagle.co.uk

BAIN DE SOLEIL

by DAVID VANN

WILLIAMS COLLEGE IN Massachusetts. 1985. I arrived in ripped jeans from California. I'd been fire-walking, meditating, learning etheric surgery, hoping to become a mystic. One of my roommates had green slacks with ducks on them. I didn't understand these pants. I never could have guessed their existence in the world. He drove a Saab 900 Turbo, had a computer that was black, with no brand name. He owned new skis and shirts in every shade of pink and blue, and he was not alone.

I tried to have friends, of course. I tried Essica Kimberly, for instance, heiress to the Kimberly-Clark fortune you see on every toilet paper roll holder. She was amused but wasn't biting.

I tried befriending Oregonians, but they were better adjusted. I tried the African-American student group, because they were all bitter about being here, but our bitterness wasn't the same. I tried a suicidal girl named Anne, but she was always disappearing and maybe killing herself.

So as the snows hit, I went down into the basement. We had a large heating unit down there, and it had a very nice hum. I closed my eyes and sang along with this hum, harmonized. I did this for hours.

I also went outside and spun in the snow, especially if there was a moon. I turned in circles as fast as I could, staring up at that moon, sometimes for nearly an hour, until I was so dizzy I no longer felt alone. I hadn't had an alcoholic drink yet, or ever tried drugs, so spinning and the heating unit were as good as it got.

But then finally, in the spring, at a campus showing of Charlie and the Chocolate Factory, I made a friend, Jamie. He taught me how to ride the unicycle, and we both moved out to the west coast. I transferred to Stanford and he got into grad school at Berkeley. That next year, we bundled up in my father's old army sleeping bag and rolled down hills behind the Stanford campus, bumping and flying and screaming, perhaps the most fun I've ever had. We unicyled all over Berkeley. We had vegan Chinese food with brown rice and laughed at pants with ducks on them.

And then, in the summer, we flew to France, and this was where everything changed.

Jamie's family in Paris had a daughter, just finishing high school. She shrieked one day. Shrieked right in the hallway and collapsed to the floor. I thought someone had died. But it was only her boyfriend breaking up with her. She screamed and howled all night, unending. I do mean that, at least twelve hours non-stop.

She was ready to chew off her own leg. The pain she felt was vicious and animal. She banged her forehead against the floor until her mother held her head back.

I didn't know how to respond, and no one was looking for my response anyway. I was becoming a loner again. Jamie was busy with his family, and I had bronchitis, was sleepy all the time, had no energy. I wanted to play my guitar, but it wasn't allowed in the apartment because of thin walls, was illegal on the street without a permit and, when I sat on the grass in a park, I found out that was illegal too. So I sat in the bedroom alone and just held it. My arms were around something, at least. I felt a bit pathetic.

I had never studied French, and Jamie's family spoke to me in English only to say things like 'You poor American boy, you have never tasted real mayonnaise.' They found me extremely annoying, mostly because I had whistled too much for the first day or two. I had always been a whistler, but most people don't like a whistler. All my years of hunting as a kid, hiking for ten or twelve hours with a gun and a dog, I had whistled, and I could do two tones at the same time, songs in harmony. I had dreams of becoming the first two-tone blues whistler. I had once gotten a third tone to come in, a low liquid, but that had happened only once, and no one ever believes me.

I'm not sure how it happened, but Jamie dumped me. He realised he was gay and left me for a guy named Duncan. I never met Duncan, but apparently he was British and promised a wider world. So I went to Quiberon, in Brittany, because it was far from Paris. I took a ferry out to some island and pitched my tent on a bare headland.

Short wild grasses, turned brown in the sun. Small wildflowers holding their own. It was a beautiful island, but the summer sun was intense, and there was no shade. Not a single tree. I didn't have sunscreen, or a hat. I tried sitting in my tent, but it was an oven.

So I went to town to buy sunscreen. A one-street village. My forehead and nose and neck stung. Even my arms and legs. I was fully lobstered. No signs that I could read, but I found a store finally, a low-roofed affair with no lights inside, very dark after the glare. I needed sunglasses, also. I had left for this trip woefully unprepared.

Wooden shelves, a very small store, and I looked at each item but found nothing that looked like sunscreen. No hat, no sunglasses. Inflatable beach balls, towels, food, wine, bread. I grabbed a jar of cornichons, my fondest memory from Paris. I waited in line, and when I made it to the counter, everyone waited. Une baguette, I asked. And then I trotted out the one sentence I had in French: Je voudrais un pain aux raisins s'il vous plait. I would like some raisin bread, please. I had to repeat it, but then the raisin bread was handed over.

Sunscreen? I asked in English.

Blank looks all around, and some sense of impatience. Sunscreen? I asked again.

Hm, I said. I was desperate. And then I remembered a brand of sunscreen in the US: Bain de Soleil. So I stroked my cheek, leaned in close, and said Bain de Soleil.

The woman behind the counter took a step back. I looked around at the other customers. I stroked my burnt cheek for them, said Bain de Soleil, Bain de Soleil. They looked at the ground.

'Bath of the sun,' or 'sun bath.' That's what I was actually saying. So perhaps it seemed I was recommending this, showing off my burn. Or maybe it seemed I was explaining my mental state. Or even that I wanted someone to give me a sun bath.

I just kept saying it, like a madman. Bain de Soleil, Bain de Soleil. I didn't know what else to do. No one would look at me. I was alone, which was beginning to seem like my natural state, something I'd never be able to run from. I had hoped that Williams College was an anomaly.

I paid for my bread and cornichons and a piece of cheese and walked out. The sun had not softened. I walked up and down that village looking for any other store, but I found none. Dirt street, no cars, access only by ferry. I returned to the store.

Cautious looks as I entered. They may have thought I would try to return the cheese, or a gnawed-on baguette. I was wearing only a T-shirt and shorts, and hadn't showered in several days. Even I felt a little suspicious of me.

I looked around more earnestly for a hat, and what I found was an umbrella. An unlikely item in a place that hadn't seen rain for a thousand years, but I was grateful. It was expensive, but I bought it and stepped outside, opened my umbrella, and felt the shade. The sting was gone. I was happy for the first time in several days. I felt that my life was turning around.

I walked out of that village back onto the headland, but I had attracted a following. A group of a dozen boys a few years younger than me. They followed about 50 feet behind, and they were laughing. You pretty American boy, they said, and they all pretended to carry umbrellas. They skipped and curtsied. They followed me onto a barren headland where there was only my tent, and I began to feel afraid. There was an edge to these boys. If I said anything, they would attack me, I believed. They were looking for a reason.

And so I went to my tent, zipped myself inside, baked in my oven, and hoped they would leave me alone.

They catcalled for a long time, and they came up and kicked my tent, batted at the top of it with their hands. They pulled out the stakes and let it collapse on me. But they stopped there. They didn't beat me, though they could have easily, with no one else around and the tent a kind of net around me. I sat there afraid and sweating and waited until there was no longer any sound of the boys, their voices and steps faded away into the distance, and then I waited some more. I cried, because I felt tremendously sorry for myself. I cried for Jamie, too, because he had been my best friend and I would not see him again.

I just didn't understand any of it. I thought of that girl in Jamie's family, how she had banged her forehead against the floor, over and over. I had never been in love, and I didn't want to be in love if it meant that. I didn't understand how Jamie could just leave me, and I wondered whether I had been more a romantic interest for him than a friend. There had been nights he had played a game, pulling the blanket and sheets off of me. I had laughed so hard my hands went weak and I couldn't resist. He'd start at one corner and just pull the blanket inch by inch, and when the blanket was gone, he'd pull the top sheet, and when that was gone, the fitted sheet, until I was left alone on my bare mattress, laughing. I had loved that game, and it had never felt sexual to me, but in retrospect it was a game that involved a bed and making me naked in a way. I wanted to talk with Jamie, at least one time, to find out his side of the story. And I didn't understand why we couldn't still be friends. Is there room for only one? If so, then that was the worst part about love.

I found the zipper and emerged from the tent. No sign of any other person. Only a light breeze, the sun a bit lower now. I was soaked in sweat, and dizzy. I drove in the stakes again, took my umbrella, and went for a hike along the headlands.

The jellyfish had come in. They were everywhere, choking the water, making swimming impossible. This promised to last for weeks. I would not be going farther than the beach. They were orange-red warning lights populating every slow rolling wave. The water cool, I was sure, and so much calmer than California. I wanted to swim, but there would be no swimming.

I kept looking over my shoulder. I wondered whether the boys might come back at night. I imagined baseball bats. And so I waited for darkness, and then I walked without a flashlight and moved my tent far away to a small fold between headlands, a place to hide, an outsider, and I hoped that this would not become my life.

NOT SCOTLAND

by ANNE DONOVAN

THE HEAT WHAUPS ye the minute ye set fit oot the plane. The brightness too – blue sky barely skiffed wi cloud.

'This is the life,' says John.

'Cannae believe this is September.' Ah pull aff ma jaicket. 'It's like the middly summer.'

Ah'd thought it'd be like autumn at hame: bright, but wi a nip in the air. Hudnae expected this.

The airport was buzzin, everybuddy checkin screens and dodgin aboot, jabberin away. Hudnae a scooby whit they were sayin. We always went tae Spain fur wur holidays and ah could make oot the soundy their lingo, but Italian was doubledutch tae me.

Boabby takes charge. 'C'moan, guys. Sergio's meetin us in the car park. Hope we'll recognise each other – it's years since ah seen him.'

'Let's hope he husnae had a facelift then.'

Sergio was sittin in a big black Merc, parked oan a double yella line. He was listenin tae the radio, wan airm restin on the rolled-doon windae. He'd on an immaculate white shirt and a fancy watch – lookin at him ah felt even mair sweaty and scruffy efter the journey.

When he spotted us he jumped oot the car. He was a wee guy, packed wi muscle; deep tan, perfect hair.

'Sergio!' says Boabby.

'Roberto!' Sergio pits his airms round Boabby and plants a big kiss on each cheek.

John looks at me and then at Boabby. 'Roberto?'

'It's ma name,' says Boabby.

Sergio turns tae us. John kinda leaned back in case Sergio started kissin him too but he stuck oot his haund and shook John's, pattin him oan the back. Then he started pumpin ma haund up and doon – thought ma wrist was gonnae break.

Boabby pointed at us. 'John… Jimmy.'

The way Sergio pronounced wur names the J sounded like a cross between S and Z.

'Whit's the Italian for Jimmy?' ah says.

'Giacomo.'

'Okay, ah'll be Giacomo then,' ah says. 'If you can have an Italian name ah can have wan too.'

'But it is ma name,' says Boabby. 'It's oan ma birth certificate – it's just cause Boabby was easier when ah went tae school.'

John says, 'So who ah'm ur then?'

'Giovanni.'

Sergio grins. 'Giovanni, Giacomo, welcome to Italy.'

✕

Afore this job come up ah'd never really thought aboot Boabby bein Italian. His ma was a baby when his grandparents had come ower tae Scotland in the 1930s. They retired and went back years ago but his da's fae Glasgow so he'd always been Boabby McCulloch. Ah never thought he looked Italian, but noo we were here ah could see that a lot of the locals had the same strong stocky build and squarish face. Boabby's Italian wasnae great but he managed to get by wi Sergio as we made the journey in the car.

Ah was dead beat efter the early start and just sat, slumped oan the leather seat, in a dwam, watchin the scenery flee by. Woods in autumn colours, small-holdins, wee villages wi orange and pink and yella buildins. When we got tae the city the traffic was mental: folk zoomin and beepin, bikes and scooters everywhere, joukin in and oot the traffic. Sergio double-parked on a main road ootside a buildin wi scaffoldin all round. He unlocked the door and there we were in a close, just like a Glasgow close, marble stairs and a coupla doors on each landin. He was bletherin away tae us, even though me and John couldnae understaund a word he was sayin. But everythin had already been arranged afore we came, wi the help of Boabby's ma.

The buildin was gettin done up inside and oot. All the apartments except wan were finished, wi new kitchens and bathrooms and all that, and we'd be decoratin them. We'd stay in the apartment that hudnae been refurbished yet. There was a big livin room wi an open-plan kitchen at wan end, a bathroom and a bedroom wi three single beds.

'That's for Daddy Bear, that's for Mammy Bear and here's wan for little Baby Bear,' ah says, shovin Boabby doon ontae wanny the beds.

'Let us know when Goldilocks gets here,' he says.

There was a layer of plaster dust all ower, but the flat had everythin we needed, and when Sergio opened a cupboard in the hall it was fulla sheets and towels and aboot fifty flowery quilts.

'They'll come in handy,' says John.

'Aye,' ah says, 'ah was worried we'd be cauld at night – bein fae Scotland, we're no used tae it.'

'Widnae want tae huvtae snuggle up thegether tae keep warm.'

Sergio haunded Boabby the keys tae the apartment and explained the complicated mechanism of the lock. He left us tae get settled, said he'd come back later and take us oot for sumpn tae eat.

✕

When the idea came up for this trip, John was all fur it, made it sound as if it was a holiday camp wi the odd bitty paintin thrown in on the side.

'They Italians are dead laid back… long lunch breaks, siesta time, nippin in and ooty cafes furra wee cuppa. Skoosh case.'

Ah knew he was exaggeratin, but ah'd nae idea how much. Noo, we're grafters, me and John, always have been, and Boabby's a good worker too. Runnin yer ain business you just dae whit hus tae be done. But here we were on the job at seven, nonstop till five. Only difference is we sit ootside tae eat wur pieces wi the guys workin on the scaffoldin. And they don't hing aboot at dinner-time, just eat their chits and get on. As for tea breaks, forget it. You can go intae the bar doonstair anytime but it's two minutes in and oot – these guys can knock back a coffee in the time it takes us tae bile a kettle.

At hame ah'm mair of a tea drinker but wan week intae the job and ah'm a convert. Doon tae the bar for a cappuccino and a bun afore we start, then another mid morn, this time wi a sangwich. In the efternoon it's a wee espresso, a blast a caffeine tae the brain that keeps you awake till work ends. Apart fae that it's watter, watter, watter, cause the weather's still like summer.

And every night we're knackeroso.

'Whit happened tae aw they siestas, Roberto?' says John. 'Ah thought everybuddy had a snooze in the efternoon.'

'Aye, right,' says Boabby. 'In the south, where it's dead hot in the summer, but no everywhere. The shops close furra few hours but they open again till late. And the workies keep oan workin. Just like hame.'

'Might a known,' says John. 'These guys are the goods but. Bloody perfectionists.'

The boss had come round at the endy the week tae see whit we'd done. And he didnae gie it a quick onceover – he examined everythin, even pointed oot a wee corner where somebuddy'd left a brushstroke showin. John was a bit narked at that; we've aye prided wursels on good workmanship and when you've been yer ain boss for a while it's hard tae have somebuddy else checkin yer work. But then Sergio turned round and said, 'bene,' and haunded each of us a rolled up wad a dosh.

'Jeezo,' said John, when we were sittin in the bar on the Friday night. They're flamin fussy in't they? At hame if you're daein up a flat tae rent oot, it's an elsie on each wall and don't be too pernickity round the windae cause the curtains'll cover it.'

'We've never been like that.'

'Naw but we've done enough jobs for guys who can barely let the paint dry cause they're wantin tae get the hoose aff their haunds. Too many of these bloody property shows on the TV.'

'Aye well,' says Boabby, 'that's wan good thing aboot the recession. Ma missus wis aye watchin thon Laurence guy, gettin fancy ideas. "Could you no stencil wee hearts roond the bedroom ceilin, Boabby?"'

Ah pat his haund. 'Aw, nice tae see romance isnae deid.'

Boabby sups his birra. 'Ah'd miss wee Kirsty but. She can relocate me any day.'

They're fussy aboot everythin but, no just decoratin. The bars and shops are clean and tidy, everythin's that organised compared tae hame. No how you expect – we think they're aw drama and chaos, but really it's no like that.

Mornins here are perfect. A wee nip in the air and a beautiful light.

The Italians turn up in jumpers and scarves. John's slaggin them aff, usin sign language.

'Bit chilly the day, in't it Marco?' he says, mimin puttin oan a big coat and scarf.

Marco pulls his airms round hissel as if agreein.

'La Scozia e molto freddo,' says John. He's pickin up a few phrases noo but they sound funny in a broad Glasgow accent. Marco nods, smiles and gets his gear fae where it's stored in the corner of the room.

Wan morn ah woke early, first light. Ah pulled oan ma kegs, tiptoed past the others and heided oot. Round the apartment it's aw busy streets and traffic but you only huvtae walk fur ten minutes tae get tae a dead quiet bit wi trees and greenery. Magic. Light and shade on the wee path, specks a broon leaves under the trees and way in the distance the sound of the city wakin up: traffic rumblin away, scraik of metal shutters hauled up fae a bar or a shop, a voice shoutin a greetin. For the first time since we'd arrived, ah was at hame here. Maisty the time ah felt like a tourist, even though we were workin. But here, in the saft light, ah felt fine.

Ah sat on a bench and thought aboot hame. What would Liz and Francis and Anne Marie be daein the noo? Only another coupla weeks and ah'd see them.

Oan the Saturday we heided for the beach, aboot hauf an hour away on the train. The seaside toon was lovely and clean and tidy, beautiful wee cafes and bars all round the front, everybuddy just walkin up and doon enjoyin theirsels.

Ah'd never been on an Italian beach afore and if it hudnae been for Boabby, who knew the drill fae his young days, we wouldnae of knew whit tae dae. The beaches here are nearly aw private, divided intae sections, each colour-coded. All you can see for miles is stripey loungers and umbrellas.

'In the summer this'd be covered in folk – it's actually quite quiet the noo,' says Boabby. He picked wanny the places and spoke to the wumman.

'Quanto per la spiaggia?'

He haunded her the dosh and she showed us a changin room and toilet, gied us sun loungers and an umbrella. We got wursels settled and ah heided doon tae the sea. Though the beach was carefully organised – neat furniture, smart towels, everythin orderly – the sea was wild. Huge big waves shoomin in, some near as big as me; in they raced, careerin ontae the flat sand, were tamed like the beach, then returned to the wildness.

It's that different fae Scotland. When ah was young and worked up north wan year in the forestry, ah spent all ma spare time on the local beach, a big empty streetch of near-white sand. Wild all through it was, hammerin agin the rocks: ruthless and dark and threatenin.

This sea's deceptive. All they smilin, laughin Italian families, kids playin a ball game on the edge of the shore, couples strollin airm in airm, cloudless sky and lovely mountains risin above the pink and white and yella wee toon. But the waves: loomin, powerful, like horsemen oot the watter, as if they could snatch ye aff the beach and drag ye away tae the fierceness of the sea, never to be seen again.

Naebuddy's swimmin, only a few folk paddle in the ripples. Ah'm staundin at the edge; freezin watter crackles round ma toes though the sun's warm oan ma back. Ah close ma eyes and breathe it in, breathe in the freshness and aliveness of it efter a week's work in a stuffy room, breathe away the paint fumes, the nights fallin intae a stupor of tiredness only tae wake in the middle of the night, nose dry fae the closed windaes. And ah breathe in somethin untamed and fresh and clean; hints of the Scottish sea so far away but nae Scottish beach ever has such heat, no even in the middly summer. Ah breathe in and oot and in again, open ma eyes and walk intae an enormous wave rearin ower me, and it hits me and blatters round me, cauld and shiverin droplets. Ah staund right in the midst of the thunderin, crashin waves as they come and go, wan minute starin oot tae sea and the next enveloped in a huge pulsin shock of watter.

FLOTSAM & JETSAM

by ALAN BISSETT

T HE SAILS OF the dhows waved on the horizon, a lazy flotilla of canvas shark-fins. Kate shielded her eyes to gaze at them, the boats conjuring scenes from the fantasy novels of her youth. She had to remind herself that these were mere fishing boats, not the advance guard of some tentacled warrior species. But here, with the cool surf nosing at her feet and the sky yawning blue, she felt dreamy and liquid, her imagination uncurling from the trap Glasgow had made for it. No bus of xeroxed minds scanning the *Metro*. No gloomy meetings at which the main word intoned was 'cuts', before – like necromancy – they'd come to pass. No clutched coffee-time huddled over the jobs section of the paper.

That morning she'd been given a lemon-grass massage by a teenage girl whose ebony fingers had pressed and kneaded out those hard Scottish knots. The girl had complained about her boyfriend's infidelity. 'You should leave him,' Kate had mumbled from the end of a long corridor, through which ambient music flowed like coconut milk.

Kate headed along the beach, tugging a linen shawl over shoulders already pinkened by sun. The sand glowed a Zanzibarian yellow. Waves hissed. Endless, sweet hours of nothing stretched before her. She'd packed big novels that needed time, space and a hammock to absorb – *Gravity's Rainbow*, *Anna Karenina* – but so far she'd lifted only a guide book which made exotic promises on each page: 'One of Africa's best known and most enticing destinations.'; 'Tropical languor'; 'Miles and miles of white sands lapped by warm, translucent waters'. Just reading it made her the sort of dizzy teenagers feel when first in love.

Further up the beach, a black man in an LA Lakers vest was chatting to a white couple wearing shades and sun hats. The couple were nodding, while the black man smiled, his fingertips pressed earnestly together. A birdsong of laughter flashed across the sand. So the locals were friendly to tourists. Of course they were. Kate reprimanded herself for fearing otherwise, then pitied those back home and their litany of excuses for not coming: Rochelle, who wasn't prepared to blow the severance pay; Harriet, struggling with her mortgage; Gerda, who'd shocked Kate by worrying openly about kidnappings, rapings, torture – 'They don't like white people in Africa, Kate. Haven't you seen the news?'

The man in the LA Lakers vest was approaching her. Kate had a point to prove to Gerda.

'How you doing today?' the man smiled, his limbs easy, his gait relaxed.

'Wonderful!' Kate beamed back, 'What a beautiful country you have.'

'Thank you. But sometimes we forget. Every day the sun. Every day the sea.' He mock-rolled his eyes. 'We need you to remind us.'

'Happy to do so.'

'Where you come from? England?'

'Scotland,' Kate replied.

'Scotland is part of England?'

'Both part of Britain,' Kate said, 'But maybe not for long.'

The man's eyebrows twitched with confusion. She sensed a long, potentially boring treatise on the constitutional make-up of the United Kingdom unroll before them, its tributary strands on Scottish independence and the vital distinction between 'England' and 'Britain' snaking infinitely away. 'Anyway,' Kate said, 'You don't want to hear about that.'

She was right. He didn't.

'In Zanzibar we want you to relax. Be happy! We have everything you need. We have beach, we have spice, dolphin, seafood–'

'Yum,' said Kate.

'We have tortoise. Very big!' At this he pretended to plod on all fours, making a thoughtful, pinched face. Kate laughed and he straightened up, then pressed his fingers together the way she'd seen him do when talking to the couple. 'How long you stay for?'

'Here in Nungwi for four days,' she said, 'then down to Kendwa, over to Tanzania on safari, and finishing off in Stone Town.'

The man nodded slowly as though taking in each point on the itinerary, then said, 'You want scuba-dive? Snorkel?'

'Um,' Kate said, 'Maybe. I hadn't thought about–'

He went into his pocket and took out a card. 'Me and brother, we run boat, take you out to sea. Coral reefs, dolphins. Ocean beauty. You like. Very good price.'

She took the card. A phone number was handwritten on it next to a name she couldn't make out.

'You stay here? In this hotel?' He pointed towards the compound, its sunloungers, swimming pool and massage benches walled off from the beach.

'Yes,' she said uncertainly.

'I look for you. Tomorrow morning. Afternoon? Take you snorkel on boat. Very good price.'

'I'll, uh, I'll have to think about that.'

'Okay,' he said, and glanced towards a man and woman ambling down the beach, 'I look for you.'

Kate put the card in her bag and watched him head towards the couple, hands open. 'Hey!' he greeted them, 'Where you from?'

The husband shook his head and didn't break his stride, the wife mumbling, 'Sorry, we don't want to snorkel.' The man wasted no further time, his head revolving, spotting another target further up the sand. 'Unbelievable,' the husband muttered.

Kate looked along the surf to see another black man – dreadlocks, Manchester United shirt – setting a course towards her with purpose. She changed direction and walked inland, but he bent his path to meet her, grinning and extending a braceleted arm. 'Hey, beautiful lady. How long you stay?'

✕

Kate blew air and waved her hat across her face, the shadow of the canopy easing her hot skin. She sipped at the mango juice and spread toes into the cool sand. Six separate men had just tried to sell her snorkelling tours on one mile of shore. She'd chatted to the first three, politely taking their cards and saying that she'd let them know. By the fourth she was lying about which hotel she was in. By the fifth she was saying that her flight was later that day. She hadn't even stopped for the sixth, instead waved him away and headed towards the sanctuary of a beach restaurant. The hawker had muttered something at her back and she'd flushed with guilt but carried on walking.

'Restaurant' was perhaps overstating things. It was three fold-down tables with straw canopies, a chalkboard menu, and a bar with two stools. Its major selling point was that when hawkers approached, the owner would growl at them in Kiswahili and they'd troop moodily away. He bowed his head to Kate and she gave him the thumbs up.

'They are not even from Zanzibar,' he grunted, 'They come from Tanzania. Leeches.'

'Oh,' she said.

He handed her a menu then left, and as soon as she looked at the menu she realised she was ravenous. Octopus, kingfish, sea bream, rock cod, grey mullet, shark, squid, tuna, sailfish. Herbs, spices, stews, curries. She wanted all of it. When the owner came back to take her order, glancing warily around for hawkers, she asked how fresh the food was.

He snorted. 'Very fresh. Caught this morning. You not see dhow?'

'Um,' she said, 'You don't get the fish from a shop?'

He shook his head, baffled at such a bizarre, foreign concept. 'Ocean is there. Reach in! Take!'

'Of course,' she said and dipped her head, embarrassed, before ordering the kingfish in coconut milk with rice and plantain. The owner smiled, gentlemanly, then retreated with a final stab of his pen on the pad.

Kate was able to enjoy the beach again, undisturbed at last: the silver line of the horizon, the turquoise waters, the drowsy spell of the dhow, the pearly waves. It was only when her eyes caught the hawkers patrolling back and forth, targeting tourists, that grit entered the idyll. They met up every so often, forming strategies, exchanging successes and failures, before detaching and trying again. She wouldn't let this irritate her. After all, she was the intruder here. She was the one who'd been picked up in an air-conditioned car at the airport and driven through shanty towns, full of houses with straw doors and roofs of corrugated tin, where children carried litres of water down dirt tracks.

Piled gloriously on the back of one of these villages: the Nungwi complex. A five-star network of hotels and leisure facilities, teeming with Westerners, which separated the townspeople from their own beach. The hotel gates had opened to her as though it were preordained from birth, uniformed Zanzibarians bowing as she'd entered. For a second, the regality of it appealed to her and she'd almost given an imperial roll of the hand.

Fuck you, global recession.

The kingfish, when it arrived, was just about the most beautiful thing Kate had ever tasted. Spicy and moist, tender and flavourful, it made the Michelin-starred chefs of Oban – a place which declared itself 'the seafood capital of Scotland' – seem like toddlers mixing ketchup with cereal.

'You like?' the owner said, as ecstasy spread across her face with each forkful.

'Oh,' she said, 'Gorgeous.'

He smiled. 'That is good. You come back here any day. I cook for you.'

'I certainly will,' she trilled, and there was a moment of hesitation when he stood over Kate's table awkwardly before she said, 'Uh, would you like to join me?'

'Thank you, that is most kind,' he said, bowing again. 'My name is Mustapha.'

'Kate,' she said, and when they shook hands she blushed slightly beneath his gaze.

Once he'd sat there was a new directness about him, as though he'd been holding back from the moment she'd stepped in. 'I am always interested in where tourist come from, why they are in Zanzibar. This is how I learn about the world. Tell me.'

'Well,' she said, leaning back from the intensity of his gaze, 'I'm from Scotland.'

'Scotland!' he said, clapping hands together, 'That is in Ireland, yes?'

'No, it's part of Britain. But it's... it might not.' She sighed. 'It's complicated.'

'You is here alone, Kate?'

She opened her mouth then closed it, scanning his intentions. But his face was earnest, with no obvious flirtation hovering in his eyes.

'Yes,' she said, 'I needed to get away. Things in Britain are very bad, very gloomy. Bad politics. Bad economy.'

'Is dictator in Britain?'

'Ha,' she laughed, 'Not quite. Almost! Anyway, I've just been made redundant.'

He creased his face.

'Unemployed. I have lost my job.'

'Ah,' he said, 'I am sorry.'

'Well, I'm not exactly the only one. The British government are cutting the public sector. So I decided to just, y'know, take off somewhere while I still have the money to do it. I might never be able to afford this again.' He was listening, but she felt an urge to sound less prosaic, more interested in his culture. 'And I've always wanted to visit Zanzibar, because it sounds so exotic and strange, and so…'

'Is beautiful place,' he smiled, 'We are very lucky for you to choose us.'

'Believe me,' she said, 'the pleasure is all mine. But now that I'm here…'

'Yes?'

'I feel a bit guilty. As though I've floated in like this rich Westerner, even though I'm not. I mean, look at how wonderful this place is, and you have tourists crawling all over it. It doesn't belong to the people anymore.'

He folded his arms and stared at her, but she couldn't work out if it was in judgement or sympathy, and she squirmed a little. 'Then why you come?'

She shrugged. 'You can't swim in the sea in Scotland.'

'Exactly. We need tourist in Zanzibar. You bring money.' He rubbed his thumb and forefinger together then laid his hand on her wrist in a brief plea.

'Yes,' she said, swallowing, 'but then I see all the poverty in the villages and I just feel—'

The owner raised a finger, his expression falling.

'Zanzibar has not poverty. Ethiopia, Ghana, Sudan, Malawi, very poor, yes. But not Zanzibar. We have tourist. We are island. We have clean water, lots of seafood, jobs, hotels, spices. Trade.'

My god, thought Kate, he thinks these are decent living standards? She considered imparting her view of the shanty towns, of the crumbling roads, of the chaotic airport where she'd had to pay a bribe to receive her luggage. *Not even the lowest-paid people in Europe live like this.* But she wondered if he might find it insulting, and held her tongue.

'Of course,' she said, 'Sorry.'

'Why you come alone, Kate?'

She glanced up sharply to find his head cocked and a curiosity boring its way in. The loneliness must've been shining from her.

'I, uh,' she found herself saying, babbling, her hands working at a cardboard beer mat, 'I don't know where my life is going. Everything feels so uncertain now. So… unsolid. Britain's becoming a terrible place. All our selfishness and greed has started to eat us.'

He was nodding, leaning forwards on the table.

'I don't know when it was that money just took over. But God, Mustapha, things feel so desperate back home. Everyone's depressed. Everyone's *empty*.' She gestured out to the sea, to the swaying dhows, to the shimmering waves, to its infinite calm. 'Whereas here...'

Mustapha ruminated upon this. 'I understand.'

'I suppose you've had greater troubles than ours, yes?'

He raised an eyebrow and took a deep breath. Then he said, 'In 1964 we have revolution in Zanzibar. Overthrow British and Arab rulers. Very violent. Twelve thousand people killed.'

'My god.'

He gave a regretful shrug, which suggested more than it stated. 'Ruler now is son of first President of independent Zanzibar. Elections not free. Police brutal. So much corruption. Did they not stop your car from airport?'

'Yes,' said Kate, remembering her driver slowing at a checkpoint and the police peering in. They'd conversed in Kiswahili and the officer had examined her there in the backseat, before waving them on.

'Is okay for tourist because tourist bring money, but we Zanzibarians have to pay police at checkpoint. Checkpoint there for no other reason. You no pay, they arrest.'

The waves rolled and hissed in the distance. Mustapha was staring at the table, a growl emerging in his voice. 'After 2000 election we demonstrate. Twenty six protestors killed by police. No one has protested since then.' He looked up at her, his face still, almost challenging.

'That's terrible,' she said quietly, 'I had no idea.'

He turned his head and stared out to sea, seeming to disappear somewhere inside himself. 'But when I was small boy here? Every day we play on beach. Every day we swim in sea. We catch fish. We laugh. We sail on dhow.'

He lapsed into silence. She reached forward and took his hand, squeezing it. He glanced up at her, attempting to smile, before he blew out air and withdrew his hand. Then he reached into his pocket.

'That remind me of something.'

'Yes?'

Mustapha unfolded a piece of paper and spread it out on the table: pictures of a dhow set against a vivid orange sunset, of blue and yellow fish, of pink and mauve coral reefs. He tapped at the leaflet with his forefinger and grinned at Kate.

'My cousin run snorkelling tour. Very good price. You like?'

AFTER DRINK YOU CAN TURN EARTH UP SIDE DOWN

by RODGE GLASS

I N THIS CLUB in downtown Hong Kong the waitresses never let your glass get below midway before offering you another drink. They all look eighteen or nineteen. They all look good. They're wearing tartan skirts above the knee and ties pulled loose over part-open white shirts, like someone's got to halfway to undressing them before deciding against it. The emblems on the waitresses' shirts read: WAN CHAI AMAZON: A WHOLE NEW ADVENTURE! As four or five of them zip between tables, talking in hand signals to punters (*You want another beer or not?*), I think to myself: we're probably the youngest men in here. Then I think: it was funny, the way Angie put it. *Our baby is born. Come and see.* Like she wanted an opinion on a new dress. Like I was expecting the news and understood. Like it's not a twenty thousand mile round trip from England to visit. Looking down, I notice my bag is poking out from underneath my stool, the panda toy and fake road sign I got at the market spilling out onto the floor. I don't bend down. With one swift kick I push them both back in the bag, the contents resting under a nearby table. Then I shout into Nick's ear.

'Lot of westerners in here,' I say.

Nick doesn't reply straight away. He's watching the dance floor, where the first few brave souls of the night are trying out their moves to Eric Clapton's *Cocaine*. Three couples are having a good time. One especially. A young local girl is slow-swaying along to the live band with a white guy in an Armani suit. Maybe he's sixty, or older. The girl laughs at something the man says, claps her hand onto his chest then lets it run down the buttons of his shirt – one button, two buttons, three – before her slim fingers rest on his belly, just above his belt. Lingering there. Her nails stroking ever so slightly, slow and soft. The guy grins. Life's just too fucking good, isn't it? When he sees me looking, he winks, like I'm next in line or something. I give him the finger but he's not even surprised. He answers by licking his lips and whipping the girl round, fast, in a circle. This makes Nick finally look away. He grabs more monkey nuts from the bowl, drops the shells on the floor with the rest and faces me.

'Yeah, yeah,' he says, readjusting his baseball cap. 'So what?'

I've forgotten the question I asked, or if I asked a question at all.

'So nothing,' I say, keeping my voice light, one palm on his shoulder as I lean in to be heard. 'Hey, you were right. Fucking GREAT band here. I mean. Just – fucking – GREAT.' These last few days, I lie without thinking. I talk without noticing. Sometimes, I don't know where I am. I wake up during the night, stagger to the hotel room toilet and think I'm already there, in my new home in the sun, Angie sleeping and the baby in the cot by our bed. Angie stirs and says, 'Sweetie, come back.' Like she used to. But here, now, I say to Nick, 'This place is a real find.' And it sounds like I mean it.

After a few songs I sneak a look at the score. No change. So I turn back. It's probably rude to check the football while these guys are ripping into *Wish You Were Here* as if they wrote it themselves, as if they're really trying to tell us something, you know? But then, it's not like we're watching the real thing. In some shitty bar next to a strip club. On a Tuesday night in April. And besides, everyone seems to be doing it. Just before they go for one last chorus I even catch the keyboard player, this guy who looks like a tribal Indian or something, craning for a view from his place at the back of the stage. But no luck: the stocky, Zen-like bass man is in front of him, in his road. One of the two guitar players is to his left, knees bent, chin to the heavens, riffing in front of the other screen. The drummer, complete with full classic rock uniform – ponytail, hair dyed black to cover the grey, skull tattoos, faded Sabbath T-shirt – is crammed at the back, his cymbals in that bit too close, blocking the smallest screen. That's the one by the exit. Or the toilet. Or both. There's no signs on anything around here. Up front, the singer and other guitar player hover at the edge of the stage – in their minds, this is a different crowd. One's doing the lead vocal, the other the harmony. Both have their eyes closed: *Oh, how I wish you were here*, they sing, crouching for effect. Then standing straight. Then opening their eyes again. The two of them, in unison. Like this outpouring of emotion, it's sudden, unexpected.

Just as I'm thinking of jumping up there and joining them, dipping and stretching in symmetry, letting the sounds conquer me too, a tartan skirt comes by, picking up two empties and looking around for more. I don't wait for a hand signal. I give a couple of my own, waving her over, then pointing to our three-quarter full bottles. She smiles, all cheeky, like I've just done something witty or interesting and I think: I could get used to it here. Meanwhile, Nick's far away. He's been singing along, his whole body consumed, feeling the thumps and chord changes along with the band as he lunges back and forth on his stool, playing the drums on his knees, his gym-toned muscles taut and visible through a T-shirt I suspect was chosen because it's ever so slightly too small. I wonder if Nick's high. I met him three hours ago. How the hell would I know what Nick's like high? Or sober? Or sad? It feels like an age before 'Wish You Were Here' finally finishes, the ripple of applause and whoops slowly dies down, and he starts talking again. Like we never stopped. Like, in this place, time doesn't pass unless Nick says so.

'These guys play here every night,' he tells me. 'Ten til six thirty in the morning. Three full sets. Can you believe that? They know, like, *six hundred* songs, man. You name it. You fucking name it. They know it. The Stones. The Beatles. *Anything.*'

Trying to keep my face straight, I say, 'They do any African stuff? I like African music.'

Nick comes in closer, checks to see if I'm just passing the time, then backs away.

'Probably,' he says, finally. 'What's wrong? You don't like The Rolling Stones?'

We've not paid for the drinks yet. I decide to play nice.

'Every night they play?' I say. 'Wow.'

Nick nods, hard. Relaxes. Smiles.

'Yeah. Well. They get two nights off a month.'

'Must need a lot of stamina. And strong wrists!'

I laugh dirty. Let him work it out.

Another few seconds pass before I take a good long swig on my drink, which is actually, no shit, called *Hong Kong Beer*. There's not even any Chinese characters on the side of the bottle. I think: this fucking place! Then I think of how far I am from Australia, and how long it takes to get there. Then how long it takes to get from the airport to the city. From the city to Angie's. From her front door to the back room, where my boy could be sleeping, right now. I try and imagine his little nose. His ears. His smell. I wonder what name she gave him, and why she didn't tell me on the phone. A wave of heat passes through me as I allow myself to hope she named him after me. I shake my head, forget where I am, then it comes back.

'These boys make a lot of money?' I ask Nick, pointing to the band with my bottle. 'This place is filling up.'

Nick laughs, snorts.

'You've not been here long, have you my little friend?'

Nick can fuck right off if he thinks I'm rising to that. I'm not even supposed to be here.

'Back soon,' I tell him, keeping it cheerful. 'Going for a cancer stick.'

Standing up, I notice the back of my jeans are suddenly soaking wet. Behind me, an old man in Bermuda shirt and shorts who can't be much less than seventy is having a good time, laughing at the cocktail glass he's just knocked over me like he's fascinated by it, like he's never seen a spilt drink before. The teenagers either side of him are laughing too. So hard it sounds like anger. The old man says 'Sorry dude,' laughs some more and says, 'Lemme buy you another one,' but shows no signs of actually getting up, doing it, or helping me dry off. I forget what I got up for in the first place.

As I clean myself up in the toilet I think: it feels like a long time since I stood at that airport gate, boarding pass in my hand, watching my connection get smaller and smaller and disappear into a paper cut in the sky. For a while, I forgot about the cost – I was just looking, looking, looking at that paper cut, a narrow slit that let a plane through into the other side of the world, my maybe future: Angie, responsibility, the end of late nights and stupid mistakes. Back in the club, I rub my jeans with a paper towel. It's not helping. I remember watching that plane leaving and thinking: I could just hide. That was a week ago. Today's the third straight morning I've got up late, hung over to hell, sat with a strong coffee in Starbucks in Tsim Sha Tsui and stared into my coffee cup imagining the little bubble in my drink is a plane, or a ship, making its way across the water. Wondering what I'm waiting for. I don't know where the days have gone. This morning, Angie's message read: *You coming or not?*

When I get back from the toilet Nick's joking with the band, between numbers, maybe making a request. I look down, and see that in among the monkey shells and the stickiness of spilt drinks, my bag has moved again. Or disappeared. Looking around on the floor, under tables, behind chairs, stumbling around blindly, I know I'm not going to see it. I remember buying the sign this morning: above a series of Chinese characters that could have meant just about anything it said AFTER DRINK YOU CAN TURN EARTH UP SIDE DOWN. A few hours ago, that made me laugh. I can't remember why. It was supposed to be a translation of something, maybe a proverb. Something wise in a Chinese dialect made silly by the English language. What did I buy the sign for? And what about the panda? Its big black eyes stared out at me, questioning.

The band are doing *Hotel California* now, the two guitarists smiling as they faithfully play out the instrumental note for note as a duo, in harmony. It sounds like the oldest song in the world. Tired, almost dead. A dead song from a long-dead age. But these boys are trying their best to bring it back to life. They look like there's nothing else in the world they'd rather be doing than playing the instrumental from *Hotel California*. The whole scene gives me a shiver. You can feel something spilling out of them, these musicians, into the room and round the whole place, the whole street, all over the Wan Chai district, throughout Hong Kong. And Nick's right with it, fist pumping in the air. When the song finishes, there's damn near a standing ovation. The singer takes off his hat, bows low and says, 'Hong Kong – you are too kind!'

'Hey Nick, these guys local?' I ask him.

'Filipino, dude. You know nothing?'

I shrug. Nick shakes his head.

'They left the Philippines together – all still live together too, in an apartment near here. And they still send most of their money home. Good boys. Fucking tragedy it is. Fucking triumph.'

'Right,' I say. 'What?'

I'm trying to concentrate on Nick's eyes, though they're spinning now.

'They went to Japan first. The Japanese are good musicians, you know, but fuck it, the truth is: their language can't cope with English sounds. Wrong shaped mouths. Good news for Filipinos! So they worked in Japan. Then here.'

Nick rubs his index finger and thumb together.

'More green,' he says. 'But still slavery.'

It feels like my turn to speak. To say 'wow' again, or give an opinion. Though I'm thinking of something else, somewhere else, I ask, 'Do they play their own stuff?'

'They could do that,' he says. 'Their songs are amazing. The best songs on this planet if you ask me. But what are you gonna do?'

He waves a hand dismissively at the crowd. I think to myself: yeah. Nick's definitely high.

'That's a shame,' I tell his spinning eyes. 'Really.' The band, I notice, is spinning too. Bass drum, spinning. Guitars, spinning. Dancers, screens, stools. All moving, in beautiful circles. Then more drinks land on our table and more empties are taken away. I don't remember drinking them.

'I understand it though,' says Nick. 'A lot of guys here are a long way from home. They want something that reminds them of what they're missing.'

'Then why don't they stay there then?' I say. 'I mean, they're just here for money, right? And to get laid?'

Nick puts his drink down hard on the table. The froth surges up the neck, over the lip of the bottle and down the sides of the label reading *Hong Kong Beer*.

'Look buddy.' He searches his brain for my name. Draws a blank. 'You know fuck all about this place, alright?' Nick clocks me checking out one of the tartan skirts zipping by. 'You come in here, spit on us and leave. You types make me sick,' he says, whispering the final word.

I don't know what that means but I do know his two eyebrows have become one bushy line that won't sit still. Why not? Why won't it sit still? His pupils are spirals. I laugh.

Nick says, 'Insult my people again and I'll kill you.'

His face is hard now, the whole thing, like it's set in concrete.

'Your people?' I say. 'I thought you were from West Virginia.'

I look around the club, thinking: I could stay here forever. Thinking: I've got to get out of here. Thinking: but where to? For a second it looks like Nick's going to boil over, frothing at the mouth, just like his beer. Like he's going to hit me. But he just downs his drink, grabs his coat and leaves. Then, as if he's planned it, the skirt comes by with the bill. Just a skirt. No smile. No woman inside. I pay and move to a barstool to watch the rest of the show.

I don't sit on my own for long. As the band kick into 'Crosstown Traffic' I feel an arm slip through mine, and a hand fall on the small of my back.

'Hello,' says a voice.

'Hello,' I say back. But quickly, 'My son is born. I'm not supposed to be here.'

'That nice,' says the voice, who also has a warm body, which has already pulled in close. Guitar Man Number 1 is changing over his instrument to one which is pretty battered, with black stains round the sides. I reckon I know what's coming. This is Hendrix, after all. The suits expect.

'I not supposed to be here too,' says the voice.

'Then what are you doing here?' I ask.

'I come to Hong Kong to make business,' says the voice and body with hands. And after a moment, 'Monkey business!'

Then a grin, a giggle. She smells like perfume, like sweat.

'I have a family,' I say. 'I'm going to see them.'

'Good. Our secret then. Monkey business?'

It's not funny, so I don't know why I smile. Laugh again. Can't stop.

'No way,' I say, still laughing. 'No more trouble. That's why they went to – '

'England, yes? I go to England. We get married. I have lots of sons.'

I finish the drink in front of me in one gulp, though I don't know if it's mine.

'No. Not England. You know what... fuck it. Sorry. I can't.'

It's hard to get words out now.

The voice and body is a girl, who looks young but old too. Her eyes say: *I know you.* Her lips say: *I know you.* Her hands say: *I know you.* She pouts, fake sad, sexy, pulling one of those little girl faces that must work on the guys out here. Seconds pass. Nothing happens.

Then she says, 'If you can't then what you doing here?'

Her voice is clipped. The night is short.

'Hey. You hear me? What you doing here?'

When I don't answer, she follows my gaze. The guy in the Armani suit is down the front now, the dance floor is full, and he's bowing down in tribute as Guitar Player Number 1 sets his instrument alight for the first time tonight. Then the guy stands, lets out a yell, looks around, and sees me again. Just for a moment. And he smiles. In his eyes, it's 1970. He's young, single, before divorce and kids and decades in sales, before escaping East to forget. Here, when he walks down the street, everyone wants to say hi. When he talks, people listen. Life's just too fucking good, isn't it? He raises his beer to the skies, mimes along to *Crosstown Traffic* and pulls his new girl towards him for one more kiss.

SEVEN QUESTIONS
ABOUT THE JOURNEY

by DON PATERSON

Why are we leaving in such unreadiness?
–Your name was last.
Is it too late to call? Is there still time to confess?
–The moment's passed.
If the weather is stormy, should we go nonetheless?
–None forecast.
Where are our dogs and our horses? Can you guess?
–Slain. Shot. Gassed.
How will we know when we reach our new address?
–Heed the blast.
How do we look in our fine new leaving-dress?
–Alone. Aghast.
Where are we going, so light and riderless?
–Nowhere. Fast.

SURTSEY

by DOUG JOHNSTONE

S HE LIFTED A handful of black sand and squeezed it through
her fingers.

There was a gurgle and she turned. He was still laid out beside
her, hadn't moved. Only the shallow swell of his chest, a thin wheeze
escaping the wound in his neck. His blood had soaked the sand, glistening like oil. There was a rattle of breath then his body slackened.

Sunlight shimmered across the volcanic vents guarding over
the island like giants. She longed to see those peaks explode,
throw ash and lava into the air like they had when the island was
born not so long ago.

She got up and pulled the broken bottle from his chest wound.
There was a sucking sound. She stepped over his body and down
to the water's edge. Through the morning haze she saw the closed

fist of Heimaey. The festival would still be going strong there. She leaned back and hurled the bottle as far as she could. It spiralled through the air and landed with a plop in the dark Atlantic.

She turned to survey the island. Ragged cliffs, dark beach, craters and cracks, all shaped into a teardrop so small you could walk round it in an hour.

So this is home, she thought.

✕

'Surname?'

'Mackenzie.'

'First name?'

'Surtsey, it's S, U, R...'

'Like the island, yes?'

She looked surprised, then nodded. 'Like the island.'

'Passport, please.'

She handed it over, pristine and unused.

'How many bags are you checking in?'

'None.'

The girl behind the counter looked at the empty conveyor belt. She had an earthy beauty, eyes like sea glass and sturdy hands. Pretty accent too, rugged and rolling. She scanned Surtsey for hand luggage.

'Spur of the moment thing,' Surtsey said, taking her passport back.

The check-in girl wasn't much older than her, maybe twenty. But she looked like she knew what to do with her life. Her name badge said 'Rán.' Surtsey wondered about that vowel.

'Enjoy Iceland, Ms Mackenzie.'

'Thank you, Ran.'

'It's 'Rown', actually.'

'Sorry, Rán.'

'It's okay, I'm used to it.'

'Yeah. I know what you mean.'

At the bar she studied the gantry.

'What can I get you, love?'

'What do they drink in Iceland?'

The barman shrugged meaty shoulders. 'Beats me.'

'Give me some Finlandia, close enough.'

He went to pour it.

'Just leave the bottle,' she said.

It was something Bogart would say in those old films her mum liked. Her stomach cramped. She waved her mum's credit card at the barman. He brought the bottle and glass. She downed it, shivered, refilled it.

She looked at the runway and wondered how many strangers would pass through the airport today.

'Just take it.'

'Mum...'

'I've got no use for it now.'

She took the Visa card from her mum. She stared at the blotches of purple and yellow where the drip broke the skin of her mum's hand. She pocketed the card.

'Take care of yourself.'

'Stop it…'

'I mean it, Sur. You have to start thinking about…'

'I don't want to, okay?'

'Please, you have to be practical.'

'Stop talking like this.'

Her mum leaned back, gasping, and reached for the mask. She held it over her mouth and closed her eyes, breath clattering. She was under six stone, her skin saggy and her stomach and bowel hacked away by surgery and aggressive carcinoma.

The descent had been quick. Abdominal pain, vomiting blood, tests, chemo and surgery, all in a month. And now this. Bedridden and clock-watching, trying to maintain comfort and dignity.

Her mum removed the mask, a string of bile from her mouth.

'Go. I don't want you seeing me like this.'

'Don't be ridiculous.'

'Promise me you'll look after yourself.'

Surtsey didn't speak.

'Promise me.'

'Where to, darling?'

She gave her address. Ten minutes later they pulled up outside. She looked at the front door. She'd spent the last fortnight alone in there.

'Wait here.'

She ran to the door, scrabbled with keys then tore upstairs. She dug around in her desk, lifted the passport and darted back out. She climbed into the cab.

'Airport.'

The driver grinned. 'Last minute holiday?'

'Kind of.'

'Somewhere sunny?'

'No.'

×

'Ladies and gentlemen, we are starting our descent. We'll be touching down at Keflavík in approximately ten minutes.'

She gazed out the window. A thread of tarmac cowered amongst jagged rocks, green waves hurling themselves against the coast. Snowy peaks and columns of white steam in the distance. Something hardened inside her as the plane swung round to meet the land.

×

'What's your name?'

She turned. He was cute, a squint smile poking through the beard. Skinny, indie, harmless.

'Surtsey.'

'Like the island? Sorry, you must hear that all the time.'

'Actually, you're only the second person ever to say it.'

He tilted his head. 'Where are you from?'

'Somewhere else.'

He held out his hand.

'My name is Snorri. Pleased to meet you, Surtsey.'

She looked at his hand. Soft skin, girlish fingers. She took it, surprised by the firm grip.

'Hi, Snorri. Fancy a drink?'

He thumbed over his shoulder at a gang of laughing boys and girls, all cheekbones and woollen wear. 'I'm with friends. Why don't you join us?'

×

They bundled from Brennslan to Kaffibarinn to Sirkus as the evening pulled focus and fell forwards. The watery daylight at midnight was dizzying and she liked it. She let Snorri's banter wash over her as she soaked up the dinky buildings, the tangy air, the singing, growling accents.

The beer garden was fenced-off concrete, palm trees painted on the walls.

'This place was in a Björk video.' It was Katrín, Snorri's friend. Not girlfriend. She was tall and solid, pointy ears.

Surtsey looked round. The place was a mess of Reykjavík's beautiful and wasted.

'Do you like Icelandic music?' said Katrín.

'Don't really know any.'

'So you're not here for Þjóðhátíð?'

'What?'

'Þjóðhátíð. The People's Festival. On Heimaey, one of the Vest-mannaeyjar, the Westman Islands.'

Surtsey stared at her. 'Like Surtsey?'

'Like your namesake, yes. You must come with us to the festival. It's the biggest party of the year.'

'Can we visit Surtsey?'

'It's illegal. Scientists only. It's a world heritage site.'

'I know all that, I meant under the radar.'

Katrín laughed. 'You could ask Gunnar.' She pointed to a stocky boy in a bobble hat and orange shades, shimmying with Snorri. 'We're going to Heimaey in his father's boat.'

'When?'

Katrín waved a hand. 'When this place dies down.'

Reykjavík harbour shrank fast as they headed southeast. They blasted through olive-grey swells, trailing white froth. The wind blew her hair, which swarmed her mouth. She tugged at it.

'Some boat, yes?' It was Gunnar at the controls. 'She's a beauty. 62-footer, 25 tonnes, but she can do 50 miles an hour easily.' He tapped a digital display. 'She's called Loki.'

Katrín appeared from below deck clutching a green bottle with a black label. It read 'Brennivín' around a silhouette of Iceland. She handed it to Surtsey, who unscrewed the lid and sniffed. Mouthwash and medicine.

'Icelandic schnapps,' said Gunnar, swerving the boat so they all had to shift their weight.

Katrín shook her head. 'Boys and their toys, eh? Gunnar's daddy is one of the bankers who brought our country to its knees. And yet he's still a millionaire. Gunnar doesn't like to talk about it.'

'Dad is an asshole.'

'An asshole who gave you his boat for the weekend.'

'Still an asshole.'

Surtsey drank from the bottle, flinched, then passed it to Gunnar. He glugged for show.

'So, how does a beautiful Scottish girl come to be named after an Icelandic island?' he said.

She'd pored over online maps and pictures as a kid. Named after an island vomited from the bowels of the earth in the sixties, a chain of eruptions lasting years. A virginal and barren land. Then, as years went on, home to tiny plants and eventually animals. A whole ecosystem untainted by human contact. She immersed herself in her mum's textbooks, revelling in phrases like tephra, breccia, palagonite tuff. She stared at photographs of lightning storms, lava flows, billowing piles of steam and ash rising miles into the atmosphere.

'My mum's a vulcanologist.'

'Sorry?'

'A volcano expert.'

'Oh. Has she ever visited Surtsey?'

She looked at the expanse of water, the mainland just a grimy shadow in the distance.

'No. She never has.'

A thick drumbeat cannoned round the crater and back toward the stage. Her eyes throbbed in time. Red flares lined the ridge, igniting one after the other, like a warning passed across ancient hilltops. People cheered as the chain of fires tore round the volcano.

She laid her head back on the grass and looked up. The same filmy midnight light. The drums stopped but there was singing from the crowd. They all knew a secret song. She tried to hear the melody, listen for the words, but the sound drifted past her.

'Are you OK?'

Snorri lying beside her.

'What are they singing?' she said.

He laughed. 'A really crappy folk song.'

She propped herself up on her elbows. 'It sounds beautiful.'

He was looking at her in a way she recognised.

'Can I kiss you?' he said.

She lifted her Brennivín and drank, wiping her mouth with her hand.

'Sure.'

She looked at the roof of the tent. The red nylon a membrane separating her from the world. She ran a finger round her nipple but it didn't harden. Snorri slept next to her, his mouth slack.

Her mobile rang, an old telephone ringtone. She sifted through her clothes, pulled it out and answered.

'Hello?' she said.

A voice at the other end she didn't recognise.

'Yeah, that's me.'

The voice was professional, resigned. A middle-aged woman tired of delivering bad news.

'I see.' It was all Surtsey could think to say.

The voice talked on, bouncing across the atmosphere between two northern countries, vibrating in the air. Surtsey waited until the woman ran out of words.

'Well, thanks for letting me know.'

She ended the call and looked at Snorri. Sweet boy. She got dressed and slunk out the tent.

'You want to go to Surtsey now?' Gunnar was swaying and laughing. Euro rave pulsed somewhere far away.

'Why not?' said Surtsey.

'Because it's illegal.'

'So what?'

Gunnar looked behind her. 'What about Snorri and Katrín?'

'They don't want to come.'

'I don't want to go either.'

'Then let me take the boat.'

'No chance.'

'If you don't, I'll just steal it.'

'You won't get it started.'

'I'll hotwire it.'

'You don't know how.'

'But I'll make an expensive mess of the electronics trying, won't I?'

He stopped dancing and stared at her. He looked round at the sprawl of drunken mayhem.

'What's it worth?'

'I'll be your friend forever.'

He looked her up and down. 'OK.'

✕

The sun was below the horizon, but fluid light still hummed in the air. She could make out the undulations of Surtsey, it wasn't far at all. Each journey took her further away from herself.

✕

She held her nose and jumped over the side. The cold pounded the breath out her body and her chest stuttered as she went under. Her head broke the surface and she gulped. She started swimming, a splashy crawl towards the island.

She felt sand under her feet and began wading. She was shivering, pushing gelid waves behind her, snot running from her nose.

She stumbled up the beach shaking and sniffing. Gunnar emerged from the water and sat beside her. He pulled a bottle of Brennivín from his trousers and opened it.

'This will help with the cold.'

They drank.

'What now?' he said, touching her hand on the bottle.

She removed her hand and looked away. Ashen beach and boulder-strewn expanses, dominated by two craggy ridges.

'Let's explore.'

They traipsed round the coast, stumbling across bulbous lava fields. They climbed a ridge, stopping at a volcanic vent. They swigged schnapps and got their breath back.

Surtsey looked out. 'Just think, none of this existed 50 years ago.'

Gunnar shrugged and eyed her. 'I need to get warm.'

'So your dad's a wanker?'

He narrowed his eyes. 'Yeah.'

'What about your mum?'

'She's OK, I guess. Not as cool as being a volcano expert.'

Surtsey shook her head then jumped up, wiping grit from her jeans.

'Let's go back to the beach.'

She lay on the sand with her eyes closed. The sun hovered on the horizon, but she was still cold. She felt his hands on her clothes, peeling layers from her. The smell of schnapps and seawater. He was rough, nothing like Snorri. He pulled her legs apart and pushed inside her. She felt the zip of his jeans bump against her. He held one of her wrists, his weight on her stomach and chest. She thought of her mum, who never made it to this desolate place. He seemed to get heavier, more oppressive. She had trouble breathing.

'Stop,' she said. 'Get off.'

She hardly even heard it herself. He grunted and kept going.

'Stop.'

She tried to prise him away with her free hand but he was too heavy. She felt around in the sand and her fingers touched the bottle. She fumbled at the neck, grabbed it, then swung hard at the back of his head. They were showered in glass. He reared up as she thrust the broken bottle at him, pushing with all her strength until the terrible weight had been lifted from her.

She revved the boat and looked back. She knew the island was dormant, but she thought she saw a tiny trail of smoke coming from one of the vents.

She steered away from the beach, the point of the teardrop. From here, the body looked like just another slab of volcanic rock, resting after the furious fires of the earth's core.

She pushed the throttle and the boat jerked forward. She pointed it away from everything and headed into open water.

PUERTO GALERA

by JASON DONALD

R UDI'S BAR SOLD the cheapest San Miguel on Sabang beach.
Their fried rice was half decent and the barmaid was perkier
than a kiddies' TV presenter. Like every bar along the coast, Rudi's
played a lot of Marley but they also put on some Clapton, the
Stones, a little Hendrix. The bar and tables were varnished drift-
wood and towards the back the sloped ceiling was propped up by
a couple of rusty scaffolding supports. Come midnight this area
passed for a dance floor. Girls twirled around the scaffolding posts
and men shuffled in their sandals. The bar at my resort hotel had
a resident lounge singer who jabbed his splayed fingers at a Casio
keyboard. Most nights I went to Rudi's.

I sat on a stool at the bar and studied the photographs stapled
above the till. Shots of bygone parties with local girls posing

on tourists' knees. Close up pictures of holidaymakers huddled together, cheering drunkenly, all teeth and sunburned cheeks.

The barmaid appeared from the kitchen and skipped up to the counter.

'Hello mister,' she said. 'I take your order?' She looked too small to work the bar.

'Hello again,' I said, taking my sunglasses off the top of my head and laying them on the bar. 'You know what? I'll just have the same as last night.'

'San Miguel and chicken fried rice?'

'You remembered.'

When she smiled her dimples formed soft slits. I wanted to suck each one right off her face. She turned her back and bent over, taking a beer from the fridge and shouted through my order in Filipino. The woman in the kitchen shouted back. A lot of the girls in this town weren't girls. You could tell by their square bony shoulders, their muscled tits shaped like apple halves shoved under their tight tops, the narrow slope of their hips. I had even seen one guy with stubble poking through his make-up. But this barmaid was properly packaged and ready for unwrapping. She placed my beer on a coaster and said, 'Sorry, we have no more chicken. You want pork fried rice?'

'Pork's good,' I said, making steady eye contact.

She flashed her dimples and disappeared into the kitchen. I sipped my beer and turned to face the breeze coming off the ocean. The bar was filling up. People drank Mindoro Slings and watched the sunset, others idly poked forks at their noodles. A heavy set man raised his hand and snapped his fingers. He pointed at his table. The barmaid hurried over with two more drinks. She gently placed each glass on the table while he stared out across the beach. As she walked back to the bar he eyed her ass, then forced his pinkie into his ear and wriggled it. I could tell he was German. Something in the bridge of his nose, the set of his brow, gave him that German look. I reckoned he was about sixty despite his green surfer's vest and wilted ponytail. The slight girl beside him was vacantly pretty. Her face paled by cream, the rest of her dark as a coconut husk. They sat alone at a table for six, up close, not speaking. His pink arm hung over the back of her chair. He stroked her bare neck and shoulder, his broad fingers exploring her ear, her throat, the corner of her mouth. Apart from sipping her drink, she didn't move. Her eyes were fixed on the horizon, watching each boat as it left the harbour. I could only guess at her age, anywhere between thirteen and twenty-three. It's hard to tell with Filipinas. Maybe she was twenty. But in the dark I bet she felt like a thirteen-year-old.

My rice arrived. I thanked the barmaid with a tilt of my beer bottle. As I ate I flipped through my PADI diver's manual and reviewed chapter four for tomorrow's exam. I memorised the symptoms of nitrogen narcosis and 'the bends' and tried to make sense of the charts for calculating decompression time between dives. When I'd had enough I pushed my plate of rice aside and lit up a cigarette. The packet read HOPE, The Luxury Cigarette! That always made smile. This country was too much.

The barmaid asked me if I wanted another San Miguel. I was diving at Reef Point first thing in the morning, but I took another beer anyway.

From behind the bar came the honking sound of a taxi.

'Is that a mynah bird?' I asked the barmaid.

'Yes sir, he belonged to a jeepney driver. He speaks the noise of traffic.' The bird hopped along the perch in the tiny cage, its black feathers glinting blue.

'What else does he say?'

'Many things.' She tapped the cage saying hello, hello, hello in a cartoon voice. The bird cocked its head and remained silent.

I sipped the beer. 'You'll just have to talk to me,' I said, smiling. 'I might even answer back.' She glanced at my mouth and she smiled too, her dimples sinking deep. She blushed and tucked a glossy black curtain of hair behind her ear. I started getting a hard-on.

'Are you on holidays, sir?'

'Yeah, you could call it that.'

'For how long?'

'A while.' I took a drag on the cigarette. 'I'm doing a dive course.'

'You like diving?'

'I like the coral reefs and the tiny fish. But I'm still getting used to the deep water.'

She looked at me.

I had an urge to tell her that sometimes, out under the waves, I'd lose sight of the ocean floor. A deepening blue extended in all directions. My breathing would pull, short and fast, through the regulator. I'd search left and right for a reference but everywhere stretched into murky nothingness. And despite the stern warnings from our instructor, I'd fin straight to the surface. Instead, I told her, 'I don't like any fish bigger than a dog. You know what I mean?'

She placed both elbows on the bar. 'I haven't been swimming since I was a little girl.'

'Really? I thought everyone here swam.'

'I have not the time. Every day I work.'

'Every single day?'

'Yes. I want to make money, go to America, but it's too expensive.'

'Don't you like it here?'

She looked down at her fingernails, began chewing her lip. 'All my life I want to leave.'

'Really?' I exhaled out the side of my mouth to avoid blowing smoke at her. 'I love it here. Seriously. You don't know how lucky you are to live in such a gorgeous place.'

The music stopped and I heard the CD player whirr and click, selecting a new disc. I finished my cigarette and stubbed it out. 'So, how much do I owe you for dinner?'

She reached for her note-pad, calculated the total, tore off the slip and placed it in front of me. I took out my room keys and wallet and laid them on the bar. The keys had a green leather tag with my hotel logo and room number branded on it. I opened the wallet, took out three thousand pesos and placed the notes on her handwritten bill. 'This is for the meal and the rest is a tip. To help you get to America.'

Her eyes widened. 'This is too much. You cannot give me this.'

'I want to.' I held up my hands, showing I wouldn't accept disagreement.

'You come from America?'

'No. Never been there.'

'Which country do you come from?'

It was my turn to look away. I scratched the label on my beer bottle as I figured out how to phrase the next bit. 'I've travelled all over, but my own country is the most beautiful. Better than America.'

She frowned and smiled at the same time.

'You don't believe me, do you?'

She swung her head girlishly to the side.

'Well, if you're not convinced I can show you pictures and clips on my laptop. You could come over when you finish work and you can decide for yourself?'

She ran a moist lower lip through her teeth as she stared at my room number, then at my wallet. I watched her considering, imagining possible outcomes. She lifted the three thousand and folded them into the pocket of her jeans. 'I don't finish work till late,' she said, her dimples gone.

'That's okay, I hardly ever sleep.'

She lifted a tray from the corner of the bar and I watched her weave from table to table collecting empties.

The German downed the rest of his cocktail and spat the slice of pineapple on to the floor. He rolled his head back and yawned straight up into the air. His girl sat passive. He leaned in and kissed her neck, his heavy arm curling round her shoulder and tickling her breast. No one took any notice. Touching became groping. She turned and playfully bit his ear then eased her way out of his arms. He laughed too loudly and smacked her backside as she left. She strode towards the ladies room and didn't look back. As I turned around to face the bar the German's stare brushed over mine. Real casual, I reached for my beer and gazed out across the bay. The sun had set. The sky and ocean were becoming the same colour, the horizon disappearing. I turned back to the bar and studied my dive book. The barmaid returned and rinsed a few glasses. Jimi Hendrix riffed through Red House. The mynah honked at bird-brain traffic offences. I was halfway through my beer.

The German appeared at my left shoulder and said, 'Give me a Slow Comfortable Screw.' He laughed out loud at his own joke. The barmaid bowed slightly and fixed the drink. The German placed both hands on the bar as if to steady it, or attempt to steer it. 'You,' he said, 'you are English, yes?' His face was potholed by long gone acne, most of it hidden under a short beard shaved neatly from ear to chin giving the impression of a jaw line.

'Not even close.'

He eyeballed me sideways. 'South Africa?' The German eased himself onto a bar stool. 'You still have the accent,' he said. He lifted my sunglasses and marked himself in the dark lenses.

'You haven't lost your German accent either.'

'You think I am German?' He snorted and shook his head.

The barmaid put his drink in front of him. He tilted his head till his neck clicked. 'It was a good country, South Africa. I was there for business in 1978, in Rustenburg. You know this place?'

'I know it.'

He closed the stems of my Oakleys and hung them on the neckline of his vest. 'But now everything is going to hell, yes? Because you allow your country to be ruled by... how do you people like to say? Kaffirs?'

The barmaid disappeared into the kitchen.

'Some people might say that.'

'Some people do say that.'

I stole a look at my sunglasses hooked onto him. 'Well, in any case it doesn't matter,' said the man. 'The whole world is finished.' He plucked the paper umbrella from his drink and the slice of fruit and the straw and dropped them on the bar. He drank straight from the glass, wiped his wrist along his lips. 'People come to this island, to Puerto Galera, only for two reasons,' he said. 'For something you can't get at home or to get away from something at home. Which one are you, Mr South Africa?'

I tasted my beer and thought about just leaving. That would be the smart move.

'Maybe, you are both, yes?'

'Look, I'm just here for the water sports.'

'Water sports? Ha!' He slapped the bar. 'Yes me also, I like very much these activities.' He pushed aside his drink and turned on his stool to face me. He nodded at my dive book. 'You have examinations?'

'Yes,' I said. 'A PADI course. Open Water.'

'Ah, only Open Water? So for you it is all new.' He leaned right into my face. 'Mr South Africa is a little scuba virgin,' he said, with a wheezy laugh. 'I show you something,' he said. From his pocket he pulled out a small tin box, laid it on the bar with a touch of ceremony.

'You go out with a boat, put on these special equipments and jump in the water. And you expect to have a good time, yes? See many pretty things. If you want you can make photos, but no touching. They are strict. They tell you down there things are delicate. Sometimes, only one touch and, paff, it dies,' he said. 'But to know a thing you must put your hands on it, feel the life on your fingers, yes?'

The mynah bird performed a surprisingly guttural mimic of an engine changing gear. He grinned and rubbed his beard, then shuffled his stool closer. 'Open the tin,' he said.

'What's in it?'

'Open and look.'

I pulled off the lid. A tiny stick of coral lay on a bed of cotton.

'When I go places I take small things, for souvenirs. Pick it up,' he said. 'This is not coral. In your hand is a pygmy seahorse. Very rare. Very difficult to find. The warts on the skin are for camouflage. Exactly the same colour and shape with gorgonian coral.'

The dried corpse in my palm weighed nothing. Its eyes black dots, the tail coiled tight.

The man's girl walked over. She slipped between him and myself, curled both arms round his waist and placed her cheek on his shoulder in a parody of sleepiness. She didn't even glance at me. 'I'm tired now, Mannie, let's go.'

'Soon, my tasty slice of cake, soon, but first I must finish with this man. He likes to look at you. What must we do about that?'

She considered me through black lashes under green eyeshadow. 'Nothing. Leave him. He's nothing.'

I gently placed the seahorse in its tin coffin and went to stand up. Mannie put his hand on the back of my neck and forced me back into my seat.

'Get your fucking hands off me,' I said. My fingers were jittery. I tightened my grip on the beer bottle. Without moving his eyes, he watched me do this.

'I know what you are thinking. Maybe that bottle will help you?' His face was broad and pale against the dark evening. 'Relax, Mr South Africa, we are only talking. It doesn't need to get ugly, not here in the bar, in front of the pretty girls. But you must choose, talk with me or use the bottle.'

I sat straighter, uncurling my fingers from the bottle.

'We were making conversation about looking and touching, yes?'

I nodded.

'And we agreed together looking is not enough. So, if you look at my wife, you want also to put your hands on her, yes?'

Saliva flooded my mouth. Though the German's lips moved, his face housed no emotion. 'Yes, you want this. You want to pull her shirt over her head and pinch her little titties. You want to push your hand down into her jeans.'

'Mannie, come. Forget about him,' said the girl. She rubbed his chest with her tiny hand.

Mannie's eyes never left me. He kept talking. 'You want to peel her panties off, bend her over and bite her ass. You wish to hold her down, to feel her straight hair twisted in your fingers and push yourself inside. Yes? Yes, you do,' he whispered.

The girl wedged herself between us. 'Mannie, bitte!'

He pushed her aside and put his face right up to mine. 'Say you want this. When no one is watching, you like to touch. Say it. Or use the bottle.'

'Whatever man… I suppose so.'

'You suppose correct. You are not so stupid as you look.'

The girl nuzzled in closer. 'Let's go, Mannie. I'm tired, baby. Take me to bed, honey, please.' She held his cheeks and stood on tiptoes to kiss him. He kissed her deep and slow then moved her aside. He opened the legs of my sunglasses and put them on his head. The girl was steering him out of the bar, but he leaned back and snatched up the tin box. 'If I see you again, I put some of you in a box.'

Arm in arm they left. Their shapes dissolving into the dark. She was only half his width.

I wrapped both hands around my beer bottle to stop them trembling. The barmaid appeared. She kept silent till I glanced at her. 'Would you like another San Miguel?'

My wallet and keys lay on the bar, my room number face up. I grabbed them and left, out the opposite exit, onto the beach. I stumbled across the uneven sand towards my hotel. The wind was thick with spray and shells crunched underfoot as I picked my way through the dark. I had to check out tonight. Couldn't have that fucker knowing where I was or how to track me down. The surf raced up and I was instantly up to my knees in cool froth. The water waited for a moment and then the undertow pulled. Grain by grain the ground beneath me disappeared. As I lifted my leg my flip-flop came off. It bobbed to the surface and gently rotated on the face of the water before being sucked out to sea. I lunged at it, splashing and chasing through the surf. I waded into the glistening black sea, up to my thighs, to my crotch, chasing it, the shoe just inches out of reach.

LAST WORD

by SUKETU MEHTA

THE OBIT EXPERT offers a service: he will write your obituary, the short story section of the newspaper. 'What if you die tomorrow?' he asks the rich, the powerful. 'Do you really want some hack on a deadline to assemble lies or unflattering facts about your life?' He will, therefore, sit with you, interview your family and friends, and pull together a 500-word obituary that can immediately be emailed to the papers on your departure; an obituary that is not a hagiography but which outlines the high points of your life, your achievements, and the family you wish to be associated with. 'After all,' the Obit Expert argues, 'you spend so much time polishing your image when you're alive, hiring public relations experts, taking care of your grooming, being careful in the interviews you give to bring out your best. Shouldn't you pay even more attention to this most important article that will be written about you? The one that will summarise your entire life? That will be, literally, the final statement on you?'

The Obit Expert's initial clientele consists of corporate heads, prominent artists, politicians, activists. But then he finds out even the little people are conscious of how they want to be remembered. Shoe salesmen, bus conductors, insurance clerks also want to arrange their obituaries. 'It may not appear in the *New York Times*,' says a wine merchant, 'but the *Wine Trades Gazette* will doubtless run a short notice, and I just wanna make sure they get the facts right. I don't want them speaking to my ex-wife.'

Obituaries are those things most people stumble upon while turning the pages of the newspaper on their way to somewhere else, just above the classifieds and after the stock market listings. Few people read them online, for how many people would deliberately click on Obituaries? The Obit Expert knows that his profession is dying, his skills will not be passed down to apprentices.

Occasionally, he accepts a commission to write, strictly for private circulation, the other obituary, the one listing the secret life. Who the dead person's loves were, the shadowed side of his heart. 'At the age of 31, Mr H fell in love with a woman not his wife. This adulterous love affair lasted with interruptions for the next thirteen years, before she broke it off. Subsequently, Mr H sought solace in prostitutes. He had another, far briefer, yearlong liaison with the lawyer Z D. This was terminated when Z D's husband discovered its existence. From then on till the end of his life, Mr H remained sexually faithful to his wife, who was never aware that he had ever been otherwise.'

Is this secret life as important as the public one? Mr H's distinguished career in the law, the many victories he won for his clients, his landmark acts of philanthropy and his civic works; where does this measure up in comparison to the anguished Friday afternoons when he had to leave his mistress, not knowing with whom she, a beautiful single woman, would spend her weekends? Which part of his life occupied his thoughts more? Which is more worthy of examination, if not of emulation?

Working on these private commissions, the Obit Expert has acquired a keen appreciation for gossip. All these people walking around the streets of the great city, secretful. Our attempt at getting at the secret life is gossip, he is convinced. Gossiping about a person is the greatest favor we can do them, because it shortens the distance between the lived life and the projected one; gossip is the bridge between us and our secrets; gossip helps to see a person whole. Oh what a relief for the person to realize that everyone suspects, and his secret is public.

In addition to running your obituary in the newspaper (and assuring good placement, and often your picture in the paper), the Obit Expert will keep a list of all your friends, family, business contacts and acquaintances, and immediately upon your demise mail in tasteful stationery the obituary to all of them, so that they know how to remember you.

These same friends, family, business contacts and acquaintances will be periodically interviewed and briefed by the Obit Expert so they know what to say if someone other than the Obit Expert calls them after your death. So he will ring up college friends, old lovers, and the neighbors and grade school teachers of your childhood, and bring them up to date on your accomplishments, your many laudable volunteer activities. He will also listen carefully as they tell him what they might have, had he been a newspaper reporter calling to get quotes for an obituary at that very moment. Sometimes, in fact, he pretends to be just that, to get the truth. After listening carefully, if there is anything to be corrected, any misperception, any lapse in recollection, the Obit Expert will refresh the acquaintance's memory. 'You say that you remember Mr H as an average student,' he will tell your high school principal. 'But, in fact, my analysis shows that he was consistently in the top one-fourth of the class where grades were concerned; he participated in numerous extra-curricular activities including track and the Young Pioneers' Club; and he was voted Secretary of his senior class. Perhaps you have overlooked these facts? After all, it's been thirty years...' Or to an ex-wife, 'I understand your feelings about Mr H after he left you for a younger woman. But consider that he was under immense stress from the failure of his business, and that he was on the road for nine days out of ten, and it is in the nature of the human animal to crave companionship.'

If that does not work in persuading your ex-wife to revise her comments about you, the Obit Expert will try something a bit more forceful: 'And, after all, it could not be said that your marriage at the time was on an even keel, even before the second Mrs H came into the picture, could it? Were there not certain tensions arising from... your lack of... shall we say, responsiveness in the conjugal arena? Did not months go by during which you failed to share your husband's bed?' If your ex-wife then screams abuse or hangs up the phone, the ever-patient Obit Expert will call again or send a letter by certified mail. 'Should you repeat these unfair and unwarranted attacks on my client when called upon by the newspapers after his death, I, acting in my capacity as the jealous guardian of his posthumous reputation, will sue you for slander to the full extent of damages permitted by law. Furthermore, I am in possession of certain material facts about your own record in the marriage, which has been far from spotless. Would your children like to hear about the time Mr H opened the door of the maid's room to find you there with the servant in a position which left no mistake about the precise nature of your relationship? This may sound like a threat but, Mrs H, I assure you that you have nothing to fear if you keep in mind only the truth about Mr H – that he was an ever-considerate husband, a fine father and provider, whom you met one magical evening at the Newport cotillion, and spent twenty-five happy years with until, through no fault of either spouse, you decided to part ways. I urge you to erase all negative thoughts from your mind, Mrs H – they will only cause you great harm in your remaining years.'

One day the Obit Expert was approached by a graying man. He came up to his office in the Financial District, opened the door, and stood there some time, indecisive. The Obit Expert looked at him across his desk. He assumed that the natural hesitation rose from the fact that the man had come here to ask for help with his obituary and, now that he was actually doing it, was actually here in this space, he was thinking: this is about death. I am going to die soon.

But it was not so.

'I want help in writing another man's obituary,' the gray-haired man said. 'I've heard that you have connections with the newspapers, you can get obituaries placed.'

'A friend? A family member who's passed away? My condolences.'

'Not a friend!' the Old Man almost shouted. Then, calmer, he said, 'He was not a friend of mine.'

The Old Man explained. The man who had passed away was a colleague, indeed a good friend from school days. They were both mathematicians. They had gone to high school, college, and graduate school together. Theirs was a friendship built on a shared wonder at the poetry of numbers. Walking around the silent streets of American university towns all night, sitting in cramped faculty offices and basements in graduate student ghettoes, they had discussed theorems and proofs like other men discuss women and politics.

It came time to submit a dissertation, and the Old Man withdrew into his office for six months, not seeing anybody, not his advisor, not his students, not even his friend. The Old Man had been working on a groundbreaking explanation for why certain irregular numbers, called the Planar-Mundt sequence, flipped polarities when they approached extreme Φ. The paper had no practical application whatever, but it was a highly sought intellectual prize. Finally, in great excitement, he asked his colleague to come over to his attic office one night. All through that night, he demonstrated his proof, the entirely unexpected ways in which he had hit upon it, and the multiple new directions it opened up in the field. After his discovery, said the mathematician to his colleague, he felt just a little nearer to God.

The next week his colleague submitted the paper under his own name to the leading mathematical journal; it was promptly accepted, he was given the prize for best dissertation, and a full professorship at Berkeley before he had left graduate school. The Old Man could do nothing to prove that the work was his; he had been working on it in secret, and nothing he had done in the field before had led up to this. He could not now submit his own work for his dissertation because he would be accused of plagiarism. He left graduate school without finishing, and drifted for a few years, finding work as a dishwasher, a junior high school teacher, and a crossing guard. He never married – he never had enough of an income to support a family. For fifty-five years he had brooded, through the silent watches of the night, on where his life could have been – he kept up with his colleague's progress as he went from honour to honour.

The Professor leisurely went through three wives, all of them young and beautiful graduate students; he jetted from conference to conference around the world, which paid for an immense library of rare books. And now he was on the verge of a painless death, lying in a room in his own house, surrounded by children and grandchildren. He had only a week left, said the doctors. All his colleagues applauded his heroism in the face of certain death. He did not wish to be kept alive artificially. 'Let me die in peace, as I have lived in peace,' he was quoted in the paper as saying.

'So,' said the Obit Expert, after the Old Man had finished. 'You want me to set the record straight.'

'I want you to do more than that,' said the Old Man, leaning forward in his chair with new light in his phlegmy eyes. 'I want you to twist things, I want you to make him look like the worst monster on earth. Make up things – bad things. I want him to be remembered in such a way that his children change their last name.'

This was a new one for the Obit Expert. He thought about it, and was excited by the challenge: to take a man's life and, by means of certain suggestions, by looking at the same basic facts in a new light and by convincing others to do the same, make a positive into a negative, or vice versa. Take philanthropy: you give me a man who has donated a vast fortune to the American Cancer Society. Is this surely not a sign of guilt, a vain attempt at atonement, by a man who has made that fortune in the cigarette business, killing many times more people than his bequest will save? Or is it a heroic gesture from a pioneering industrialist at the very end of his life, a modern-day Carnegie who accumulated a vast pile through some-times questionable means only so that he could give it all away to the poor; a kind of trustee of the people's wealth, wisely accumulat-ing and administering it for the good of the multitude?

And, not for the first time, the Obit Expert thought of himself as a shaper of memories of the future, of memories yet to be born of facts that lay like unformed clay, waiting to be shaped by the artful hands of recollection.

The Obit Expert accepted the Old Man's assignment, and set to work gathering and cataloging facts about the Professor's life.

He did not have much time – the death was days away. He gathered all that had been written by or about the Professor, and it was considerable. He spoke to his colleagues, his friends. Then he interviewed his two ex-wives, posing as a newspaper reporter (and indeed, there were other journalists out researching his life for favorable articles that were daily being written about the dying laureate – out researching, even, in case the worst should happen, an obituary, the replacement of which with his own version would in itself require the Obit Expert's utmost effort). One evening the Obit Expert looked at all the piles of paper, all the computer records, all the interview tapes in front of him on his desk. It would be most difficult.

The Professor seemed to have led a singularly blameless existence – even his ex-wives spoke well of him, understanding that his towering genius needed more than one partner for its inspiration. He had helped younger mathematicians win fellowships, teaching positions. His children remembered him as a loving, if sometimes distracted, father. And his fellow mathematicians, all save the Old Man, spoke of him in terms reserved for the likes of Euler and Ramanujan – 'the most significant mathematical mind of the last half-century' and 'a thoroughly original approach which will change topography forever'. Princeton was waiting to rename its Mathematics faculty after him. And not one of them – not his peers, not one of those that survived of his mentors, not his students – alleged or even suggested that he had ever taken credit for work not his own.

The Obit Expert knew that there was only one man remaining on earth that could provide him with the information needed to destroy the Professor's reputation.

It wasn't very difficult to get into the house. The suburb in which the Professor lived had no fear of the adjacent city. The Obit Expert simply climbed into the Professor's ground floor bedroom through the half-open window. A solitary nurse was asleep on a chair, holding in her lap a newspaper with her horoscope.

The Obit Expert stood in front of the Professor and said the Old Man's name.

Slowly, the Professor's eyes opened.

The Obit Expert said the Old Man's name again.

The Professor was smiling now. 'Is it time to go?' he asked the Obit Expert. 'It must be time to go, because you've come, you who I've been waiting for all these years.'

And the Obit Expert held the Professor's hand as he went.

OTHER TIMES,
OTHER PLACES

by JOAN LINGARD

M Y HUSBAND'S BROTHER picks us up in the car bought for him by his mother in Toronto. We are going first to the outskirts of the city, to a Soviet-style housing scheme. My brother-in-law wants to show us his home. Before we start to climb the four flights of unlit stairs he removes the window-wipers from his car. One cannot be too careful. They will steal anything round here. And who can blame them when they have so little? My husband warns me to stay in close to the wall. The handrail is missing in places. A skylight provides only a little illumination on the top landing. When we reach it my eye is drawn to a jagged hole in the wall. My brother-in-law shrugs. There was a shooting last weekend. He thinks his neighbours could be drug-runners.

His wife is waiting to receive us. We present our gifts. Small, decorated tins of tea, packets of women's tights, various other items of clothing, bars of soap, pairs of Clarks real leather shoes for the grandchildren, a couple of ghetto-blasters. All excellent articles for bartering. My husband's suitcase is empty now. We can leave that with them too.

They show us their two-roomed apartment and tell us how they shared the bedroom with her father for many years until he died, while their two daughters slept in the living room. They have no hot water. They live frugally, on the state pension, and have no savings. He was an anaesthetist at the children's hospital before he retired; she was a doctor, a specialist in radiography. They could have earned more driving tractors.

After we have drunk our tea we set out. We are going on an expedition into the country. We travel slowly. The roads are full of potholes. There are few cars and no buses. In the fields tractors rust, but it is summer and the gentle rolling countryside looks benign and beautiful. The birch trees are in full shimmering leaf, reminding us of our beautiful Speyside. The hedgerows are speckled with flowers of many colours. The people love nature. They revere it. When the family came to meet our train from Leningrad their arms were full of flowers.

At midday we pull up in front of a collective farm. My sister-in-law consults with me in poor German. Neither of us speaks the other's language but we manage. I open my bag and she selects a tin of tea. We wait on the sunny roadway while she disappears round the back of a large wooden building. When she returns she is smiling. We can have lunch! We have not seen any restaurants since we left the city.

We are seated at a long wooden trestle table. The farm workers are already eating, dipping their chunks of bread into bowls of thick stew. They seem not to be unduly curious about the new arrivals. My sister-in-law insists on serving us. We are treasured visitors from the luxurious west and we cannot be expected to queue up with farm workers for our lunch.

After we have eaten and before we travel further we must visit the facilities. My sister-in-law apologises profusely before we reach them. They can be smelt on approach, reminding me of campsites in rural France where we spent summers with the children in years past. I used to hose down the latrines before I let the children set foot in them. Here, there are no hoses. When I come out I wipe my shoes on the grass. My sister-in-law apologises again. I tell her not to worry, it is not a problem.

We travel on.

Our destination is no more than sixty or so kilometres from the city but, on arrival, we feel as if we have travelled a long way. We come first to a small town. Some of its old houses are wooden and badly in need of repair, though still occupied. The whole country is in need of repair.

The house stands three kilometres outside the town. The childhood house of my husband, designed by his father, who, until the Second World War, was City Architect of the capital. After the first Soviet invasion he was denounced as an Enemy of the People, like anyone in a position of authority or who owned land. He was forced to go into hiding. My sister-in-law's father, a farmer, was exiled to Siberia. In 1944 my father-in-law took the decision to flee the country, taking with him his wife and four children. They became refugees, blown across Europe, like leaves in the wind, hither and thither, until they made landfall in Canada four years later. The eldest son, who is with us today, was unable to escape and ended up a prisoner on the island of Sakhalin.

I stand at the gate and look at the house, a beautiful, imposing building of yellowish stone, with a semicircular balcony and a colonnaded portico beneath. The garden is overgrown, which distresses my sister-in-law, who loves to grow flowers and vegetables. During the occupation the house was commandeered and given over to six families. There are only three there now, one on each floor. My brother-in-law does not know the inhabitants of the basement and ground floor but he is acquainted with the elderly husband and wife on the first floor. The husband taught mathematics at the local high school while his wife was a dentist. They have remained there throughout.

They welcome us warmly. He takes my husband into another room and shows him a chair. He says that he thinks my father-in-law designed it and would my husband like to have it? He is a little embarrassed. My husband takes the chair but later gives it to his brother. We go into their father's studio. It is crammed with furniture from various rooms in the house and reminds me of an auction sale room. In the dining room murals by one of the country's leading artists grace the walls.

We go into the sitting room and are offered coffee, along with birch juice and dandelion wine, both home-made, and ginger biscuits. As we raise our glasses to wish each other good health my husband murmurs to me that these were his mother's sherry glasses. They are delicate and finely made. I feel a shiver up my spine but when I look sideways at my husband I see that he is calmly sipping his wine. They have endured much more than the loss of sherry glasses in their lives.

After we leave the house we visit the churchyard, where grandparents have been buried. It is a real country churchyard, with simple headstones and flowers growing around the graves.

We drive back to the city in the early evening. The western sun mellows the countryside, turning the birch leaves to golden. The birds are in full-throated song. Before my brother-in-law drops us off at our hotel we stop at the Freedom Monument. A newly-wed couple has also stopped. They get out of their car and lay a wreath of flowers at the foot of the monument under the stony gaze of two armed Russian soldiers. The people are becoming bolder. There is a whiff of revolution in the air.

Our hotel is a soulless, newly-built high-rise, but adequate, and the toilets flush. We take the lift to the eleventh floor, gliding smoothly past the second, where it never stops. On that floor the blinds are permanently drawn, behind which men and women perform their secret service activities. When we emerge from the lift we pass the two women seated at a desk who stare impassively through us and we through them. Our return has been noted. We go into our room. We do not speak of our day in the country, of our lunchtime visit to the collective farm, or the house where my husband lived as a child. We have been warned. Remember, one cannot be too careful. There are bugs everywhere. My brother-in-law will only speak of his experiences on Sakhalin out in the air, away from walls.

That was 1989.

The hotel has since been modernised, westernised, and the windows on the second floor are no longer blinded. The city is alive with restaurants, slick cocktail bars and tourists who are free to come and go as they please.

My brother-in-law lies in the country churchyard; his widow lives in a city apartment. After the revolution the family claimed back the house and my brother-in-law and his wife lived there for some years, enjoying the garden and the peace of the countryside. The lodgers remained in the basement and on the first floor. It was desperately cold in winter. Heating was inadequate. Pieces dropped off the balcony rail. The roof needed renewing. The family could not afford to renovate the house. It has now been sold, along with the valued murals and most of its contents, to a property speculator. I cannot help wondering if the sherry glasses were included in the price.

HORROR STORY

by KIRSTIN INNES

T HE HOTEL FELT like a place where bad things had happened, she'd decided. Something chilling about the uniformity of its too-long Soviet-functional corridors, their flickering lights. She'd pulled the shower curtain back sharply on the bath in the first room they were assigned, having seen vague dark shapes piled behind the damp-spotted opaque. Bodies, she'd thought, severed limbs, maybe.

– It is only moss, her roommate had said, bending over and poking the dirty khaki growth covering half of the enamel. It was the first time she'd spoken, although they'd come up in the elevator from the foyer together; Claire hadn't actually realised she could speak English. They'd stood together in the bathroom's damp air, eyeing each other.

✕

Vasvija's head was shaved close all over, dark fuzz prickling out. All week, she'd worn the same green velour tracksuit top, its pile sticking out from her skin at the same angle as her hair, like a wolf on the defensive. She kept a sharp, feral smell zipped into it. Underneath – Claire had seen her out of it twice, now, and they'd been sharing a room for four days – she wore the free t-shirt handed out by the conference organisers, a t-shirt they designed for men, in clashing colours; that big ugly logo screened cheaply over her wide, flat chest. Her eyes were massive, startlingly pale in her head, too, and there was something strange clouding them. Impossible that they were the same age – she just didn't look like people Claire knew, at home.

– Well, we'll need to ask for another room, Claire had said, in the bathroom, on the first day. We can't wash in that. It's not hygienic.

Vasvija had grunted, picked her frayed boy's backpack up off the bed she'd marked as hers, and plodded out into the corridor.

✕

The curtains were drawn in the second room, which seemed to be fizzing with static as the light went on. The manager flicked his head at the window and said something fast. Goran translated, anxiously.

– He says there is a. There will be. Much noise? There will be men, working outside. Because you are female you will need to keep the curtains closed.

– Building site, said Vasvija. There is a building site.

All three of them looked at Claire.

– Okay, she said. She tried to smile at the manager, put her thumbs up. He just wheeled off, back towards the lifts. Goran looked even more worried.

– You will be at lunch in an hour?

He ran after the manager. The door slammed, shutting Claire and Vasvija in together. The hair on Claire's arms prickled.

– I just felt that we couldn't wash in there, she said. In my country, it's okay to complain if you don't like the room. Sorry. I'm sorry.

Vasvija flopped down onto her bed.

– Okay, she said, and put her thumbs up, before turning her back and curling herself into the wall.

They'd been welcomed onto the stage with bagpipes that night, at the launch – apparently it was a Serbian instrument too. That familiar wheeze and drone, the pitch, and then it tipped into something twisting and Eastern. Music to charm snakes to. On the ceiling of the hotel's shabby function room, a huge chandelier began to pick up the whine, each overly ornate arrangement of crystals shaking.

– Well, I've never heard the bagpipes played like that, Dr McKenzie muttered to Dr Wood, and they chuckled together, rich meaty men's chuckles. Goran stepped up to the microphone, his fat smile back in place again.

– Visiting all the way from Scot-land! he'd said, then something in Serbian. Dr McKenzie, Dr Wood and Claire had turned their heads one at a time, at the words that sounded most like their names, and made their way to the stage to smile and wave. Goran had said something else and the pack of young Serbs who seemed to make up the majority of the conference had laughed, clutched each other.

The delegates, from Slovenia, Croatia, Macedonia and Serbia, were almost all her own age, she'd noticed, roughly under thirty. Claire had only been asked to two conferences before, but she still knew this was unusual. It was like a whole generation of academics had just vanished. Dr Wood and Dr McKenzie were the oldest delegates there, apart from a big, silent Serb, Dr Maljikovic, whose hair hung greasily over his face, skin grey and covered in cold sweat, his eyes wild. He was the only delegate not to have provided an English translation of his work.

– His name actually is Igor, too, she could imagine herself telling Jamie, back on their sofa, and they'd laugh about it together.

The nightmares hadn't started until the second night, but they were the worst sort, so realistic she wasn't sure they weren't true. Sometimes it was the corridors, but more usually she was in the room itself, and there was another presence there, something animal, something lurking in the corners of the room, shuddering, whimpering to itself to lure her in. She'd always wake up just before it pounced, sweating in the man-made fibres of sheets she was pretty sure hadn't been changed since they'd arrived, to hear Vasvija breathing jaggedly, darkness pooling in the corners. In the mornings, the threatening ape-cries of the builders outside woke her up long before Vasvija's alarm clock.

She wasn't getting much sleep.

– It's spooky, this hotel, isn't it, she'd said to Dr Wood, after she'd sat with him at breakfast one morning, and he'd nodded down at her.

– Typical of the Yugoslav Soviet style, of course. 1960s.

He reached across her for the coffee pot.

– You know, of course, that it was the Serbs who came up with the idea of the vampire?

She shook her head, and he looked pleased with himself, warmed to his theme, her lecturer again.

– Oh yes. Vam*pyr*. The bloodless being. Invisible.

Four days in and their room was heavy with the smell of Vasvija. Claire suspected that she had her period, because of that metallic, iron-rich undernote. The curtains stayed closed and no fresh air was getting into the room; humidity levels were at an all-time high for the area apparently. Claire could feel her clothes wilting.

Vasvija didn't even seem to wash. Really. Claire had bought litre bottles of mineral water from the kiosk in the main square and lined them up along the bath after she'd turned the tap on in the second bathroom, after the pipes had growled and coughed up viscous yellow liquid and she'd choked on its sulphur stink, after Goran had assured her that the water was just like this in this town, it was perfectly safe to bathe in, and they couldn't move rooms again, and Vasvija had begun to avoid her eyes as they moved around the cramped space between their beds.

– I just don't think it's reasonable to ask us to live like this, she'd tried to say. I mean, it's practically third world, my god! The rest of the town – the rest of the country isn't like this, surely?

Vasvija's face was suddenly turned to hers, the space between them gone in a jump-cut, as though her roommate had moved at superhuman speed. Her words hissed through tiny, pointed cat's teeth.

– Please, can you stop complaining? Please.

Those huge eyes.

Vasvija was from Bosnia. She hadn't volunteered that information herself. Dr Wood had mentioned it to Dr McKenzie while Claire walked beside them to the conference room.

– It's a huge gesture, of course, for them to invite that Bosnian girl here, what's her name, Vasvija Cerić.

– And for her to come, Dr McKenzie had agreed. Extraordinary.

Claire waited, but neither of them turned to her and said – and of course, you're sharing a room with her, aren't you?

Bosnia. She knew something had happened there, but it just meant half-watched news reports from her teenage years, really.

Footage of refugee camps, girls with pale eyes in headscarves, a charity album they'd all bought at school because Damon from Blur was on it.

X

That weird heat still hung in the air, even though the sun had gone down, clothes shucking sweatily to backs. The delegates sat under awnings outside a bar in the square, noisy from the pleasure of being out of the hotel, the pack of young men snapping at each others' heels, joking in the foreign spikes and lilts of their language. Goran was in the centre, crowing like a cockerel as his acolytes applauded and thumped him on the back. The big, frightening Serb, Igor, sat just apart from everyone, staring over, with a bottle of something strong-smelling. There were no other women there, although she'd tried to extend an invitation to Vasvija, when she'd gone to the room to pick up her jacket. It was the first time they'd spoken in two days.

– I do not want to drink in a bar with Serbian men, Vasvija had said, pulling the covers over her head.

Claire was buying her own drinks. Beer, although she didn't usually; it was easier just to go up to the bar, point at the tap and hold a single finger up. It sat heavily in her belly, and she kept turning her head away from the stilted conversation she was involved in to expel the gas behind her hand. She hoped it would just look like she was yawning.

She'd come along to the bar because there had been nothing else to do, because it wasn't the hotel, because she'd loosely thought about flirting with one of the men for a little pleasure, for that small sexy glow. Perhaps even a kiss to take with her under the blankets when she eventually had to go back to that room. None of them had paid her any attention, though.

– We are mostly engaged in translation, Miho, the clever-faced Croatian, was saying. When we are not teaching students, or writing our own books, my wife and I are running a publishing company, translating works of American and English literature.

Claire nodded, tried to swallow another burp.

– Your English is excellent, she said.

He looked at her for a second, and there was something familiar about his eyes.

– Yes, he said.

Not thank you, she thought, how funny.

One of the Serbs knocked his chair over as the mass of voices got louder, and suddenly, English, rising over the top.

– We should ask the British woman, hey!

The smirking boys pushed in around her table.

– Hey, hey, Claire. In England, when you are telling a man he is a pussy, is this a very great insult?

He was quite good-looking, the one who'd asked.

– Wouldn't know, mate, she said, twinkling at him. I'm Scottish, not English.

– There is a difference? he said, returning the twinkle, teasing her.

She went for the laugh, feeling the alcohol move, slack in her.

– Oh yeah! It's probably like telling a Serb he's Croatian.

Around her, eyes widened. Goran stood there looking like he'd forgotten his smile was still on.

– I don't think you mean that, Miho said, quietly.

– This guy! Goran shouted, pushing through shoulders to the table. I love this guy! He seized Miho in a sideways-on hug and kissed his cheek. Miho looked politely at the table. Some of the boys around him made a Wooooahhh noise. Igor stared over at them, pushed his chair very forcefully back and walked off down the street, leaving a sour-sounding whistle in his wake.

– I'm sorry, she said to Miho. I'm sorry. Evidently I said something inappropriate.

– I think perhaps you don't understand very much about the history of these countries, Claire.

Well, she could only be honest.

– No. No, I don't. I mean, I do know that it's a good thing that you're all here. That you came, that my roommate, Vasvija, came from Bosnia –

He smiled a bit there, relaxed again.

– It is an important thing for us to be friends, we of this generation.

– But it's an extraordinary, eh, gesture, isn't it? Your countries were all enemies?

– Is it not just as extraordinary, then, that a Serbian invites British people to his conference?

Claire didn't get it.

– I'm Scottish though, she said.

The smile again, under the faint black fuzz of what might be a moustache.

– Scottish pilots can still fly bomber planes, he said.

– I'd better go, she'd said at the floor, had practically run down the hot, dark street with her cheeks flushed. Goran had called her name anxiously, had hurried down the street after her. She'd been touched.

– Really. I'm just tired. I know where I'm going. Have a good night.

She walked for a while, quickly, conscious of the sweat pricking her, of the air tightening in around her.

It's not my fault, she should have said. I didn't know. That's why I'm here, to learn, she could go back and say to the table, cut over their drunken shouts.

She didn't, though.

The building in front of her had been painted pink once, probably about ten, fifteen years ago, but it badly needed a new coat. An old, bald politician stared crisply, sternly from a poster pasted on the wall, a red anarchist A carved into his forehead.

In fact, the poster seemed to be the only thing holding the wall up. It wasn't just the paint: the bricks and stones of these buildings seemed to be peeling away under the air, flaking off, drifting down into piles of masonry dust in the gutters.

Around her, the town waited, silent, pending something.

It was coming; she could smell it.

Claire began to run in what she thought was the right direction. The streets were empty, all the shop signs in the Cyrillic alphabet, that strange code she couldn't hope to crack, only the odd word breaking through. AUTO. SALON. TEENAGER DISCO!

Somewhere behind her, a low growl echoed off the pavement. Her muscles prepared for flight.

A flash of light, and the hard shock of something on her skin. Rain. Lightning. A storm.

✕

The hotel foyer was completely abandoned – no-one at the desk, two lights out and a third flickering ominously. The space felt charged, primed, full of electricity, and Claire thought of the static-crackling curtains in her room. Her finger had been hovering automatically at the elevator call button, but she ran for the staircase. Rain-noise battered the building, its tempo changing as she reached the first floor. It sounded wetter, nearer, as though it was coming from inside the hotel – from inside the conference room. Claire pushed open its heavy door and saw, through the gloom, water leaking, cascading down through the fittings of the chandelier. And all the lights were flickering. Flash. This whole building could turn lightning conductor, she thought, every plug socket loose and ripe for potential treachery. Charred flesh sticking to the melted nylon fur of the blankets.

In the hallway by the dining room she could see motion, hear moaning. She approached almost without wanting to. Igor, the big Serbian, stretched out in one of the leather-covered massage chairs left for guest use, mechanical hands groping his writhing muscles. His eyes were closed, his mouth almost obscenely open.

– Igor. Igor. Dr Maljikovic! You should get out of the chair. I don't think the hotel's safe. The electricity –

As the lightning flashed again, his eyes snapped open. He tried to stand and move towards her, groaning, but his arms and legs were clamped by the machine, and she took her opportunity to run, taking the stairs two, three at a time, until she reached her floor, where all the lights were already out. She struggled with the key in the lock of her room for agonising seconds before she broke in, could slam it behind her.

The television was on, and the room lit strangely – she felt the static more than ever before, and it took her a while to realise that it was coming from the window, that the curtains were open. And there was that noise, the raw whimpering of her nightmares. It was coming from the chair in the window.

– Vasvija?

Nothing, just the noise.

– Vasvija. I think we ought to switch the television off. There's a leak in the building. The storm.

Vasvija whipped round in the chair, as the lightning flashed again, illuminating her face, her eyes red.

Oh god, thought Claire. This is it. This is it. That thing was Vasvija. It had always been Vasvija –

– You're back, her roommate said, her voice thick, blank, full of snot. How did you enjoy the bar?

She blew her nose.

Vasvija was crying. She was sitting in the chair, watching the storm, crying, curled up and tiny. Claire's heartbeat began to slow, a little.

– Ehm. Are you okay? Is it the thunder?

– Fuck the thunder, Vasvija said quietly.

– Sorry?

– Fuck the thunder. My. My friend – my lover. She no longer wants to be together with me. She tells me this by SMS message, this evening. The whole time I am in Serbia she does not want to answer my calls, and then only she sends this fucking SMS message! This is all I am getting! We are together three years and this is all I am getting!

She looked into Claire's face, then, and she laughed, a simple, bitter, human laugh, a laugh that said shit happens.

– Claire, you are looking as terrible as me. What has happened to you tonight?

Claire thought about home, about watching telly on the sofa with Jamie, about eating pizza. Her easy, easy life, doing well at school, slipping straight from undergraduate to postgraduate at the same university, saving up for the wedding, not suffering. Not at all.

– I. I just don't like thunderstorms, she said, finally.

Vasvija did that laugh again, but it wasn't unkind.

– But you are from Scotland, she said. You have a lot of storms, no?

Claire exhaled, staggered to the bed, sat down.

– Not like this, she said. Nothing like this.

SASSUOLO

by ELEANOR THOM

T HE NAME, SASSUOLO, made me think of holes, cheese full of holes. I never saw any holes, but they must have had to dig somewhere because they needed clay. The place made millions of tiles. There were factories all over the countryside, and it was hot, hotter still with all those furnaces going and all that dust which got up your nose.

The dust, and the fried meat Adriana served twice daily, made me drowsy, and in between servings I'd go to my room and sleep. Sassuolo was a half hour away and there was no bus. I felt a mess anyway. I had conjunctivitis. I'd had a whole month of that with the Vaccaros, fried meat, dust, and the sound of the slippers they made me wear, rubber soles slap-slapping between the dining table and my bedroom. Bare feet ruined terracotta. Adriana said.

She was stupid about things. She washed her dishes twice before stacking them in the dishwasher, and because my bedroom backed onto the kitchen, she often woke me while she handled crockery and hung cookware from the rack on the ceiling. She had a maid she liked to scold while the two of them scrubbed the frying pans.

It was about then, a month in, when they decided to do something about my boredom. We were at the table. A strip of beef had just slipped from the frying-pan to my plate, and the small television in the corner was tuned to MTV Italia.

'Adriana. Salt,' said Signor Vaccaro.

She pushed back her chair and returned to the cooker, picked up the grinder and set it down beside her husband without a word. He grated a layer of salt onto his portion of oily beef. Signor Vaccaro was the reason I was with them. He was five foot tall and fat and balding, and I was his au pair. *His* because all the Vaccaro children, his two sons and her daughter, had grown up and left home. I was supposed to be teaching Signor Vaccaro English in return for my bed, my fried meat, and a pocketful of lire from Adriana every week, but so far, he wasn't interested.

'Are you bored yet?' Adriana asked. At first she had tried to talk to me about the Royals, but she had given up with this by now.

I said my eyes were getting better. The conjunctivitis had been so bad that every morning my lids were glued shut and I'd had to paw my way to the bathroom to soak them open. But the infection had made me sleep, which passed more time. That was a benefit.

'You should do something with her. She's your *inglesina*,' Adriana said to Signor Vaccaro.

He shrugged and chewed his meat.

'She likes animals, don't you?' said Adriana.

This was how the visit to the stables came about.

The Vaccaros had an Alsatian cross with a long, rough coat, and they kept her chained to a tree. There was also a short-haired pup that scampered around the patio and cried at the kitchen door. I had a soft spot for the pup, even though it had given me the conjunctivitis. I'd let him in my room one night, thinking it would comfort him and he would curl up and go to sleep, but instead, not long after I turned out the light, I saw the shadow of his little tail lift, and heard something running onto the floor. He had messed all over the terracotta, both ends. I had to put him back outside and clean up before Adriana found out. She loved those tiles more than anything.

The pup was free to run around. It was the other dog I felt sorry for. The week I arrived I bought a lead so I could release her from the chain and walk her around the houses. We did a circuit every evening as soon as it was cool enough, and sometimes I'd stop to stroke her coat. She was rough with dust. The streets were empty and the houses were modern, hidden behind electric gates. In the gardens there were figs, lemons and olives. The figs were in season and they were delicious, but illicit. Fierce dogs hurtled along the fences, guarding the fruits.

I thought Signor Vaccaro would be driving us to the stables, but the two of them were waiting outside the front door. Both cars were still in the garage. They were doing this for me. They had deduced from my routine with the dog that I liked to walk. Signor Vaccaro was dressed in a dark purple shell suit, and Adriana stood beside him, towering over him in stilettos with white jeans and a multicoloured Moschino shirt. Her hair was an out-the-box red and tightly permed, dried upside down. They made an unusual pair in their matching bug-eye glasses. I walked ahead and the Vaccaros took turns behind me, her crippling on the dusty paths, him sweating in his shell suit.

When they caught up with me they asked questions. They were curious about my love life. I kept the details to myself, but there were already three boys that summer, all friends of the Vaccaro sons that had been introduced to me the Saturday I arrived.

The first took me to Reggio Emilia one evening, where we walked around the medieval buildings. It was dusty there too, and all the shops and cafes were shut. He talked about history and his work, and he took hold of my hand, which I didn't really want. I had just finished school, and I thought he was too old to be taking my hand without asking first. Later we stopped at a restaurant and took a table outside, next to a couple who were sharing a mozzarella. It was a whole mozzarella, round and white and slippy, and it lay between the man and the woman like some silken thing that together they had just spun. They petted over it, peeling layers and slowly feeding each other. My date complained that I didn't look at him while he spoke. He must have been used to better attention, but I couldn't stop watching the other couple, gazing at each other as they skinned the moon.

I was pleased when the first boy left for America a couple of days later. He brought a yellow rose to the house and handed it to me in front of the Vaccaros. They insisted I keep it, and hung it upside down to dry so it would last forever.

The second boy took me up a winding road to a country club
with a pool. Our swim kits were rolled into towels and slumped
like swaddled babies on the back seat. The boy talked and grinned.
When I think of him now I think of teeth. On the straighter sections of road the boy would take a hand off the wheel and try to
dip his fingers up my short skirt. I felt like telling him it was not
on. It was like going to the cinema and trying to grab popcorn
from someone else's bucket, but I didn't have the guts to say that.
Instead I crossed my legs, looking out of the side window, and
when we got to the pool I refused to go in the water. I kept my
miniskirt fastened and read a book.

Marcello, the last one, was a bit different. I liked Marcello and
he liked me. The Vaccaros probably guessed this easily enough
because I would speak to Marcello on the phone. But I didn't tell
them. I didn't go into details.

At the stables, Adriana's stilettos stabbed through manure and
muck, and she bent over to try and brush the red dust from her
white knees. We looked into the stalls. They picked out a beige
horse, and I was taken to a room to try different helmets. Adriana
watched me swing into the saddle while Signor Vaccaro stood staring into the distance. Clouds of dust were rising from tile factories.

'She doesn't ride like an *inglesina*,' said Adriana.

Riding was hard work in the heat, but I was pleased to be away
from the house. I stayed out for nearly two hours. The Vaccaros
waited. When I got back they were leaning with their armpits hooked
over a wooden fence, tipping their bug-eye glasses to the sun.

They didn't know this, but I had gone through their spare cup-
boards in my bedroom. Most of it was Adriana's winter clothing,

fur coats, cashmeres, ski salopettes, silver moon boots. At the bottom of the cupboard there were piles of old magazines with pictures of the British monarchy on the cover. The Royals stood rigid in front of palace gates in navy coats, silk ties, fancy hats and grey suits. Proper *inglesini*. But it was in amongst these magazines that I found an Italian translation of a sex manual. I sat on the cool terracotta and flipped through it. There were line drawings of a couple doing it in different positions, him on top, her on top, thighs swung around thighs, and just about everything else except for back to back. There was a chapter on all the ways a woman could lick a man's hard-on and, if that got dull, how to tie bows and beads around it like it was a poochie dog. Maybe Adriana did that with the Gucci scarves she arranged around her neck. She'd want to paint it with nail varnish and sweep eyeshadow over it too. Adriana liked presentable. I put the book back, making sure to bury it deep, sandwiching the cocks somewhere between Adriana's beloved Diana, The Queen, and the blotchy faces of Princes William and Harry.

Marcello was shy about his thing. A few days before, we'd been in the park, lying on the grass. When it got cold he had snuggled nearer but kept fidgeting his hips to hide how much he liked me. I didn't mind. He told me about his mum scratching his back. She used to scratch it for him when he was a little boy, every morning before school while he lay in his bed. He spent an hour with my hands. He manipulated each finger till it tingled, making circles in the skin of my knuckles and kneading warmth along the fleshy parts of my palms. My hands felt different afterwards, flexible, like he had dipped my bones in honey.

He needed to go home to fetch a jacket. Marcello lived in an apartment near the main road. He lived with his mother. They didn't have a garden or a dog, and the apartment had a narrow hall with five or six doors either side of it. Between two of the doors there was a glass cabinet full of trophies which shone gold and silver in the dim glow from the lamp on the ceiling. They were Marcello's trophies. His mother was proud of them so she kept them on display. He saw me looking at them. He told me he won them for Italian dancing, when he was a little boy. I wanted him to demonstrate but he wouldn't. He said there wasn't space.

Marcello opened the door to his room. It was small with a single bed and the covers were pulled back and rumpled. I could imagine him as a boy, lying face down with his head on his arms, and his mother waking him up, scratching his thin, pink back. He picked up a frame from a shelf behind the door and showed me what he looked like when he danced. The boy in the picture wore a green suit and looked about nine years old, exactly how I imagined him. Marcello put on a jacket and tucked a wallet into his back pocket before we went back out for the evening. At some point later he went into a bar and asked for a pencil, and he wrote the address of his flat in the little blue book I had bought from a museum in London. We could keep in touch after I went home.

My legs ached after the horse-ride, and the walk back to the house was uphill. Adriana hurried far out in front, stepping wide to manage the path in her stilettos. I held back. It was one of those evenings that just didn't cool off, and I could hear Signor Vaccaro stepping behind me, struggling for breath. He had to take a rest every few paces.

'Are you alright?'

He didn't have the wind in him to answer, but nodded and waved me on. He seemed to smile, for just a second, and then without a sound the smile fell away. Signor Vaccaro collapsed. He went kind of sideways onto his knees, then toppled back. It was fast. No noise or fight for breath. He just went down and that was it. I looked at him curled in the dust, his eyes closed but his mouth open, with some vowel sound left unsaid, stuck like a peach between his lips. 'Ah', he seemed to have wanted to say.

Ah.

'Adriana!'

I shouted three times before she heard. She made a strange, high-pitched noise of surprise, and started immediately back down the hill to see for herself what sort of a state he was in. She called him directly a few times, but he lay so still he could have been dead, and when one of her heels came off at a jaunty angle she stumbled and twisted her ankle. She kicked the shoe across the road.

'Die killed,' she screamed at it.

She gave up after that. With one stiletto still on her foot she tripped away like a three-legged greyhound, back towards the house where she could telephone for help. I suppose that was quick thinking.

Left alone, I unzipped the top of Signor Vaccaro's purple shell suit. The bug-eye glasses were in his hand and he was clasping them very tight. I took my cardigan from round my waist and made a cushion under his head. I checked for a pulse in his neck. There were drips of sweat running down him, wetting his collar.

He didn't look pale, but then I supposed he wouldn't. His skin was so deeply tanned you could almost call it a hide. It reminded me of a goatskin bag I'd bought at Camden Lock. I remembered the stall holder telling me he bought them in the Middle East. They were his bestsellers.

I found a pulse, but I couldn't tell if it belonged to me or Signor Vaccaro, and I couldn't think what to do anyway, apart from rolling him onto his side and tipping back his head. I moved a leg forward and made sure his chin was lifted off his chest. I thought it would be good to roll him into some shade, but I couldn't do that alone, so instead I sat beside him with my hand on his shoulder. I watched for cars and listened for the siren. Adriana's stiletto lay in the gutter like a pistol.

The ambulance and Adriana arrived at the same time. She had changed out of the white jeans, and on her way down the hill she stopped to pick up the shoe and put it in her handbag. They had a mask on his nose by now, and they had rolled him onto a bed which raised and lowered on silver wheels. Adriana handed me a key.

'Is this your daughter?'

Adriana explained that I was just the au pair, and she took the young paramedic's hand and let him help her into the ambulance after the bed. Inside, the paramedic began explaining what they were doing to Signor Vaccaro, and all the time she kept hold of his white-gloved hand and used the other to cross herself. The doors closed behind them.

I had my collar between my thumb and forefinger. It was a superstition, learnt on a school trip. If you see an ambulance, clutch your collar until you meet a four-legged creature. The ambulance left. I watched till they swerved onto the road at the bottom of the hill, and then I just stood there in the silence. All I could hear was the Rottweiler in the house opposite, panting through the bars of the gate. I let go of my collar.

I was at the airport within a couple of days. Signor Vaccaro was still in hospital and I'd hardly seen Adriana since the walk. She got her maid to drive me away in her small, white Fiat that smelt of cleaning cloths.

'You missed your mamma?' she asked me.

'Yes.'

She said she had a daughter about my age. 'You are pleased to be going home early.'

When she dropped me off she said '*Buon viaggio, Inglesina.*'

I told her my name.

'They always called you *Inglesina.*'

'I'm Scottish, really,' I said. 'I just live in England,' and she laughed so hard she had to prop up her sunglasses and wipe her eyes.

It was too early to check in. I blew a good deal of my lire on a phone card, and rummaged in my bag for the little blue book. I spoke to my parents and my friends from school. I couldn't wait any longer. I wanted to know if it was sunny in London.

Two hours later I was eating a tricolore salad from an Alitalia dish. Tomatoes, avocado and pure white mozzarella. I wondered what I would say in my letter to Marcello. I felt bad at leaving without a word. I'd never told him I liked him. I strung a few sentences together in my head but, some seconds later, at an altitude of about thirty thousand feet, I realised I couldn't write to him anyway.

I was so excited to be going home that I'd left my little blue book at the airport. I knew exactly where it was. I could picture it. It would be sitting there now for someone else to find, all loose pages and scribbled addresses, and Marcello's neat, pencil handwriting. Propped open on top of the payphone.

CHICAGO

by ALLAN RADCLIFFE

I<small>T'S DARK WHEN</small> we leave the bar. The rain has stopped and the air is hot and damp, garbage-sweet. Beneath the streetlights the sidewalk gleams yellow, the ground a mosaic of footprints.

'You're not with anyone?' He has to shout over the traffic noise.

'No,' I say, too quickly. Close-up he looks younger than in the bar, maybe early twenties. His skin is beach-coloured, his cheeks and nose dotted with freckles. Dark eyes and thick, black eyebrows set strikingly low on his forehead giving his face a melancholy look even when he smiles.

'Your name?' His tone is clipped, like a teacher taking a register.

'Alex.'

'Al – ex.' Then, almost as an afterthought, he taps his chest. 'Tomas.'

We cross the river and swing between the traffic on Wacker Drive. The town is heating up. Tomas strides ahead. I have to jog to keep up with him. I ask him where he's from. 'Chile.' He smiles at me expectantly and I try to dredge up everything I know about Chile, but all I can find are names: Allende. Neruda. Pinochet, for fuck's sake.

'And you? You are from Chicago?'

I blurt out a laugh. 'No. Scotland –' My voice rises to a question mark, but Tomas bobs his head emphatically. 'Oh yes! I visited Scotland once with my family when I was fourteen. Edinburgh... Loch Ness... It's beautiful.'

'I'm from Glasgow –'

'Ah yes, Glasgow. The plane landed there, I think.'

Tomas's hotel overlooks the river. The name of the hotel is embroidered in silver letters across the front of a wide awning that extends all the way to the edge of the pavement.

In the bright foyer Tomas clicks across the polished floor and holds out his arm, palm up, smiling like an old friend. The man behind the desk bows his head as he holds out the key. As Tomas strides across to the lift, nodding at me to follow him, the receptionist catches my eye and holds my gaze, blank-faced, aloof.

Tomas's room is at the end of a long, wide corridor. The door opens onto a narrower passage with closed doors on either side.

'Washroom in here.' He pushes at one of the doors and flicks on the light, waves his hand vaguely in the air. The tiles and tub are bathed in the same golden light as the hotel foyer. The bathroom is the size of my room at the hostel.

I follow him into the bedroom, transfixed by that bit of him where his long, brown neck meets the collar of his shirt. One end of the bedroom is all window: the glass is filled with smooth, black sky and the pointed upper reaches of the buildings opposite. The centre of the room is taken up with a king-size bed. Two framed photos stand on the bedside table: Tomas with loved ones, faces jostling for attention in their line-ups, effortlessly pushed into the background by Tomas's lens-filling smile.

'Drink?' He drops to his haunches and scrutinises the minibar.

I slide apart the glass doors and step out onto the balcony. The airless heat pushes against me. So much for the Windy City. I look down and my stomach dips. The hotel and its neighbours converge so close to the river that the water makes a protective moat around us. Patient queues of cars edge over the bridges. The river is black, streaked silver. Across the water a train creeps towards the station. To my left, the traffic shoots frantically up and down the freeway. Chicago. I grip the railings, tip my head back, lean back, letting my heels take my weight, a smile stretching my face.

Tomas hands me a plastic cup of red wine and the rest of the small bottle. As he taps his glass against mine I accidentally let go a cackle of pleasure. He looks at me quizzically, touches my cheek with the back of his hand, opens it into a palm and lays it against my face and neck. He drops his hand and gives my shoulder a little squeeze, then takes a long pull of his drink, leans against the railing.

I sip my wine. 'So what brought you to America?' His eyes narrow. 'The States, I mean –'

He sighs deeply as though it's too boring to go into. 'Oh, I have just finished my studies –' He looks out at the city, his eyebrows knitting and unknitting. 'I have the choice of going travelling or spending the whole summer working in a telecommunications company with my friends. My father gave me money to go travelling.' He frowns. 'I don't think I can go back for a while.'

Tomas started his trip in California. I mention some places, but he just smiles at me indulgently and nods, non-committal. San Francisco? 'Yes, it is a nice enough place – very beautiful, colourful houses.' Los Angeles? 'This is really a difficult town I think, very dirty. I was scared to go out at night.' Las Vegas? 'What can you do there apart from push money into machines?'

I think back to my long weekend in Vegas. There was a boxing match on, the town was heaving and the hotels on the Strip were all booked up. I ended up in a place miles from the centre called Relax Hotel, full of weekending families. The pool overflowed with children.

'But the people are nice here, don't you think? Friendly?'

He hesitates for a long moment. 'Some of them.'

Then he lifts his head, steps forward and wraps my hand in his, says something that starts with, 'I think we should –' and leads me into the bedroom.

There's no fuss with Tomas. He cups my face in his hands, pulling me towards him, so close I can see the thin, dark line of tomorrow's stubble emerging around his chin and upper lip. There's no give in his waist when I put my fingers there. Just hip bones jutting out, hard as handles. The skin on his hands and neck is soft and there's a pleasant metallic taste on his tongue.

He pushes me gently onto the bed, arches over me and puts his hands on me, runs his fingers all the way from my cheek down to my waist, pulls me close, fits himself to me. By the time we're lying kissing with our hands inside each other's clothes I've settled on what I always do: improvise, act, pretend I'm someone else, a character in a film or from the television, someone who knows exactly what he's doing.

Later, we lie side by side on the bed not saying much. I ask him if he's all right and he smiles and nods. 'Yes. Very.' He yawns and unravels his long, lean body, turns his head towards me. The bed is so wide I have to stretch out my arm to touch my hand to his. Tomorrow a shyness will open up between us as we reach for our clothes, negotiate who's going to use the bathroom first, attend to our hangovers, try not to notice each other's imperfections.

I take him to a busy café near Grant Park, a grungy place. Tomas glances around warily, clutching his canvas messenger bag to his side. We sit on an ancient, threadbare sofa so low his chin's just about resting on his knees. This makes us both laugh. I ask Tomas if he's been out on the scene much in the States, and he just wrinkles his nose.

When the breakfast arrives we sit in silence, reading the different sections of a newspaper. Occasionally Tomas laughs or snorts and shakes his head and opens the paper to let me read whatever article he's taking issue with. He laughs wildly at one in particular: Obama claiming the banking system is sound. As he reads down the page he wipes the tears from his eyes, like he's watching a sitcom.

At some point his mobile buzzes and his face bursts alive. 'My brother.' He shakes his head, beaming, his smile widening as he scrolls through the text. 'His daughter had her third birthday party.' He laughs. 'Can you believe it? Thirty other children and their families were there.'

He lays his phone on the table and gazes dreamily out of the window, his eyes narrowing at the sun, his face slowly sagging.

'Have you just the one brother?'

'Mmn? Oh no.' He leans forward. 'Two brothers and two sisters and me. Five.' He taps his chest. 'I'm in the middle.' He counts off his siblings on spread fingers. 'Boy, girl, boy, girl, boy. My father says we are like a seating arrangement at a wedding. Here.' He thumbs the keys on his phone, hands it to me. 'Look, here I am with my niece. Pilar.'

In the picture, Tomas is cradling the white-wrapped, sleepy-eyed newborn baby in his arms, laughing, open-mouthed.

'She's cute. Does she live in Santiago too?'

He stares at me. 'She lives in my home. We all live together.'

'You live with your brother?'

'My brother lives in the family house with –' He counts on his fingers again, 'His wife and me and my parents and my little sister and my little brother... My older sister lives with her husband and family.'

'In Santiago?'

'Across the street.' He tucks his phone in his pocket and shrugs. 'This is normal for Chile.'

'You must have a big house.'

'Big enough for all of us. The servants also live in this house.' He lowers his eyes, self-conscious suddenly. 'Many houses have servants. They are like members of our family.'

He lifts his coffee. 'And you? Tell me about your family.'

'One brother, one sister. She's in Italy. Tuscany. She teaches English there. He lives in New Zealand.'

He clatters his coffee cup into the saucer.

'He works there.' My voice comes out hushed, apologetic.

'And your parents?'

'I... one of each.' I laugh weakly, but his face is wrinkled in confusion.

'Your parents are alone then?'

'I –'

I picture Mum and Dad sitting in their armchairs in the living room, smiling at something on the television, and a wave of sadness goes through me, a pressure building against the backs of my eyes and nose. They dropped me off at the airport three months ago. Dad kept asking if I was okay for money. 'Remember to phone when you get there,' Mum said repeatedly. 'I'll just feel so much better when I hear your voice.' I didn't get round to calling them until three days after I arrived. Mum was frosty when she answered. 'You're obviously having fun, then.'

Tomas stares at me, his brow grooved, like I'm a tricky clue in a crossword. I set my face, suddenly childishly angry. His eyes drop to the floor as if drawn to some fascinating detail on the carpet.

Out on the street Tomas looks at his watch and sucks at his teeth and frowns.

'Well –' He flattens his palm to his forehead, screens his eyes from the sun's glare. He leans in my direction, as if about to follow me.

'I'd better get to work.'

He shrugs. 'Maybe I will see you later –'

'I –' I hesitate for a moment, unsure what to say. He's surprised me. 'Um...'

His eyes narrow further. He has long, stiff eyelashes like a girl. 'Sure, why not?'

I write down the address of the pub I work at on the café receipt, and tell him to come at about six.

There's a baseball game on. The regulars huddle around the television, the low chatter occasionally broken by cheers or defeated groans. In between serving drinks I clean and polish the bar, sweep the floor, wipe the bar stools and restock the fridges. I try not to watch the door.

Tomas arrives at quarter past. He looks too tall for the small, cosy pub. He walks straight over to the bar, smile slanting from cheekbone to jaw.

I tap my watch. 'What time do you call this?'

'I have to make myself look my best for you –'

'If that's your best –' Emboldened, I aim an open-lipped kiss at his mouth. As I pull away, he laughs, almost involuntarily.

A groan from the television area: the Cubs are four-three down. Tomas stares into the corner with an expression of open-mouthed wonder on his face, an anthropologist who has just stumbled upon a hitherto undiscovered tribe. His eyes linger momentarily on the group in the corner, who are shaking their heads into their beers, and then he turns back, his eyebrows raised in wonder.

×

We take the bus back to the hostel so I can shower and change. Weary-eyed passengers sit or stand quietly, staring at the floor and the roof, just as they do on the underground in Glasgow. Rain drums against the window. Tomas complains loudly about the lack of decent weather in summer in Chicago, as though he's been short-changed by the travel agent. People are turning to glare at him, but he rattles on, oblivious.

To distract him from the weather I tell him something I've been saving up, a story that has come back to me, about an exhibition I saw a few years back, photographs of Chilean refugees living in Scotland. Now I only remember images and half-stories, but I do remember one account quite clearly, that of a musician who was imprisoned and tortured in the National Stadium. This stuck in my head. It seemed so wrong that a sports stadium could be used in such a way.

And I'm telling him all this, and at the same time I can hear my voice getting faster, climbing up the scale. 'It's terrible,' I keep saying to Tomas, 'It's just so... terrible.'

And I don't know whether it's because I'm talking too quickly or if the sound of the rain slapping the windows is making it hard for him to hear me, but he doesn't really respond. He just smiles distractedly into my face as though he's only half there.

My room at the hostel is narrow, barely a person's width: a single bed with a roof over it. Tomas has to duck to get under the door. I watch him stepping gingerly over the debris of underwear and socks I left on the floor two nights ago. He sniffs the air, pulls aside the pale green curtains and opens the window. 'For the fresh air,' he murmurs, confronting me with wide, innocent eyes like a kid who has been caught doing something he shouldn't have.

I go to the showers, and when I come back Tomas is stretched out on my bed, peering at the dog-eared copy of Kitty Kelley's biography of Frank Sinatra I picked up in a hostel near the Grand Canyon. He's about ten pages in. I sit down beside him with my towel wrapped around my waist and another towel round my shoulders and shake my wet hair all over him. He laughs and throws the book onto the floor, catches my hand.

We sit on the bed leaning against each other for a while. Tomas asks me if I think North American men are good-looking.

'Their teeth are mostly very nice.'

'You have many boyfriends here?'

'No.'

'You don't have a boyfriend in Scotland?' he says.

I shake my head, smiling, remembering the song my mum used to sing: I've a laddie in America and another in Dundee-aye-ee-aye-ee –

I squeeze his hand. 'What about you? No boy back home?'

His grip loosens. 'I had a boyfriend for a while when I was at the university. Victor. His name was Victor.' He lowers his head, his mouth turning down at the corners. 'But a friend of my family told my father. And my father was –' he closes his eyes at the memory, 'so angry.'

'Oh, I'm... I'm sorry.'

He slowly shakes his head. 'I don't think my father will ever understand.'

We both stare down at our hands. I fail to think of something to say that won't sound flippant or uncaring.

Tomas breaks the silence with a deep sigh, lifts his head, pushes his shoulders back and smiles at me.

'So –' he says, placing the flat of his palm on my chest and running it all the way down to my bare belly.

After a minute or two of kissing me on the mouth and all down my neck, he gently nudges me away, slides down his jeans and pulls his T-shirt over his head.

We're both quite thin, but we struggle to fit comfortably into that narrow bed. We have to hold on to each other to stop one of us falling out. Laughing, we struggle to get comfortable, clinging on to each other like we've got one air supply between us and if we let go we'll lose it.

TAKE ROUTE SIX TO THE OCEAN

by AMY BLOOM

PROVINCETOWN IS A small town on a sand-bar in Massachusetts. On one side is the harbor, on the other side the dunes and
the ocean. Thoreau wrote that it was 'a filmy sliver of land lying flat
on the ocean, a mere reflection of a sand-bar on the haze above.'
It hasn't changed much in 150 years, geographically. The Pilgrims
have come and gone (pretty quickly – they wintered in Provincetown and went on to Plymouth). The Portuguese fishermen and
their families have been in town since whaling ended more than
a century ago and fishing began and they are there still, although
the fishing isn't great anymore. (You can whale-watch, however,
or hire someone to take you fishing for a day and catch bluefish
and striped bass, while watching out for the pleasure of seals and
the annoyance of drunks in motorboats.) The painters and poets

and novelists came and stayed, from Robert Motherwell and Norman Mailer to people who post their rhyming poems in the back of the pizza parlor or paint on cardboard because they can't afford canvas. Gay artists came with their straight siblings, and once the artists and their shifty, sexy ways cleared a path, gay accountants, gay plumbers, gay businessmen, gay schoolteachers, gay waiters and gay electricians began arriving. They, too, have stayed. And the handsome, muscular guys, all dressed like oversized toddlers, and the swaggering butches, and the two moms and two dads with two kids, and the boa-wearing queens, and the sulky teenagers all flood Commercial Street, moving like a motley wave around the German tourists and the straight families from Idaho, all of whom want their picture taken with the Cher lookalike on a scooter.

You can't buy a basic pair of pants or a plain button-down shirt in P-town. But you can buy:

- Really good oysters. (You can even just get a bucket and drive over to the Wellfleet flats and dig your own.)
- A huge, wall-covering oil painting of a man with enormous green eyes, done by a local artist, inspired by Jacques-Louis David's *Leonidas at Thermopylae*.
- A hammock woven in rainbow colors.
- Custom-made stained glass in the manner of Frank Lloyd Wright or Andy Warhol.
- A Japanese teapot made into a vase.
- Caramel cheesecake saltwater taffy.
- An antique cabinet from the Gansu Province of China, circa 1850.

· Lemon grass bath salts.
· A superb one-hour massage with a transgendered
  body-builder.
· Cranberry-walnut fudge.
· A diamond-studded vibrator.
· Blueberry-banana gelato and a blue striped sundress to
  go with it.
· A straw fedora with a black and red grosgrain ribbon.
  (Men will look dashing; women, insouciant.)
· A La Vie Boheme t-shirt. (Also one that says Your
  Gaydar Should Be Going Off Right… Now.)
· An elaborately pretty (or suitably manly) henna tattoo
  that will last two weeks and make the middle-aged feel
  that life has not entirely passed them by.
· Home-made brownies, $1 apiece, sold by the two little
  girls on the corner, in front of their house.

When I was growing up, my parents took me on exactly three
vacations. The first was to my Uncle Izzy's chicken farm in New
Jersey. I got bitten by a chicken and had to carry warm, dampish
eggs to the kitchen. After making scrambled eggs, my aunt stepped
a few yards behind the house and killed a chicken for dinner. She
wore her blood-spattered apron all day. The second holiday, we
went to a cottage on the Jersey shore. It had no indoor plumb-
ing, no air-conditioning and no window screens. I got a rash that
lasted for weeks. The third time, we went to Puerto Rico; I was
13, my sister was 18, and on the first day we disappeared for 8
hours to go joyriding with a pair of good-looking thugs. When we

got back, the Puerto Rican State Police surrounded us and then we went home. That was it for family vacations.

I was determined to give my children the holidays I didn't have (funky charm, social diversity, bookstores and toilets) and I was determined not to be one of those miserable brood-bound souls shlepping whiny children to places they didn't want to go, ending with a dropped ice cream cone for them and a drinking problem for me.

Provincetown is our place; heaven for them, and heaven for me. We drive up narrow Route 6 and there are the dunes and sky, undulating elegantly on our right. It doesn't look like what it is – the slow, destructive process of erosion. It looks like the world before people tarted it up. On our left are the small seashore cabins, which we're happy not to stay in. They're close to the dunes but have Route 6 passing right in front of, and behind, them. We pull into town and head east. We can stop at the supermarket at which everyone (drag queens, famous designers, tattoo artists, Provincetown's mayor) shops and, amid the grandmothers in outrageous t-shirts and adopted Chinese toddlers and visiting European teenagers dressed for St. Tropez, we buy vacation food. Lucky Charms cereal and peanut butter. This for the gluten-free, that for the lactose-intolerant. Diet Coke and blueberries for everyone. An inflatable raft it will take an hour to blow up.

From time to time we have stayed in Provincetown's inns (from the oddly ornate, full of damask and brocade, to the bravely threadbare with mismatched pillowcases and broken dressers) but when the guys we loved sold The Commons to open a hotel in Florida, and the tiny blue attic bedroom was no longer available for my youngest daughter, we moved on to renting a house.

The beach on the bay side spreads out toward the long arm and fist of Provincetown, the true land's end, and south towards the more polite and tidy Wellfleet. (No tawdry shops with giant sunglasses, bejeweled flip-flops and hair clips shaped like naked women.) You can walk out nearly a half mile at low tide, and we do. My daughters do the water tricks they have been performing in the bay for twenty years – handstands and cartwheels – and they do them for their niece who, at two, is fascinated but wary. We all walk down Commercial Street for pizza and ice cream at Spiritus. We go to Tom's Used Books (but only four at a time – it's not very big). We all return to the beach, hour after perfect hour. A Brazilian couple, darkly tanned and glittery in their tiny white suits, walk their tiny white bichon past us and then retreat to their muslin tent. The two older ladies bring their complete kit for the afternoon – iced tea, two crystal glasses and a tray of lemon squares. A family of three blond parents and four brown children fly a pair of kites. An old man in a sarong and a pith helmet comes by with his metal detector. The sun sets like a wide red hibiscus over the water and all of those people stop and watch it blossom and drop.

'Hallelujah,' the old man says.

The Elsewhere collection was commissioned by the Edinburgh International Book Festival, thanks to a generous grant from Creative Scotland and the Scottish Government's Edinburgh Festivals Expo Fund. In an innovative publishing and design partnership, Glasgow-based publisher Cargo and San Francisco-based publisher McSweeney's have produced the Elsewhere box set of four themed volumes.

EDINBURGH INTERNATIONAL BOOK FESTIVAL
Commissioning editors: Nick Barley, Sara Grady, Roland Gulliver
Copy editors: Jennifer Richards, Oisín Murphy-Lawless
Thanks to: Amanda Barry, Andrew Coulton, Elizabeth Dunlop,
Helen Moffat, Nicola Robson, Kate Seiler, Janet Smyth

edbookfest.co.uk

CARGO
Publishing director: Mark Buckland
Managing editor: Helen Sedgwick
Thanks to: Alistair Braidwood, Martin Brown, Rodge Glass,
Brian Hamill, Craig Lamont, Anneliese Mackintosh, Gill Tasker

cargopublishing.com

McSWEENEY'S
Design and art direction: Brian McMullen,
Adam Krefman, Walter Green
Illustrations: Jack Teagle
Thanks to: all at McSweeney's

mcsweeneys.net